Facets of Indian Diasporic Writings

Edited by

R.P. Pradhan

Supriya Shukla

ATLANTIC

PUBLISHERS & DISTRIBUTORS (P) LTD

Published by
ATLANTIC
PUBLISHERS & DISTRIBUTORS (P) LTD
7/22, Ansari Road, Darya Ganj, New Delhi-110002
Phones : +91-11-40775252, 23273880, 23275880, 23280451
Fax : +91-11-23285873
Web : www.atlanticbooks.com
E-mail : orders@atlanticbooks.com

Branch Office
5, Nallathambi Street, Wallajah Road, Chennai-600002
Phones : +91-44-64611085, 32413319
E-mail : chennai@atlanticbooks.com

Reprint 2018

Printed in India at Nice Printing Press, A-33/3A, Site-IV,
Industrial Area, Sahibabad, Ghaziabad, U.P.

Dedicated to

Sh. Manoj Sinha
Minister of State for Railways

Preface

With three million people of the Indian diaspora residing in the U.S.A. alone and with thirty million scattered world-wide, undoubtedly India and Indians have carved a niche for themselves across the globe. The cliched term "brain-drain" is no longer acceptable as diasporic Indians have established themselves in almost every arena in alien lands, making their country proud of their abilities and attainments.

Likewise, Indian diasporic writers are persistently augmenting world literature, enriching it with multiculturalism, post-nationalism, post-colonialism, post-modernism, etc. Globalization has thus created a new class of immigrants and expatriates. These transnational writers, though global in outlook, are local in habits and deeply rooted to their native country, taking up issues of their land of birth in their writings. In this odyssey to foreign shores in the quest for better opportunities it is but natural that these migrant writers, whether they are first generation immigrants who have spent a part of their lives in India and then moved to other countries, or the second generation who belong to the educated elite of India—all experience the dilemma of in-betweenness as well as the issues of dislocation and relocation which results in a perennial research for identity. These issues have become topics of extensive research being taken up by their Indian counterparts back home.

The book, *Facets of Indian Diasporic Writings* is a compilation of essays by eminent literary scholars who have delved deep into several aspects of diasporic writers and their works and sensibilities. Shiv Govind Puri discusses how Ramanujan, one of the earliest diasporic writers, though deeply rooted to his native land, simultaneously accepts living amidst different cultures and explores the aesthetic values of hybridity and globalization. He does not consider himself to be an expatriate as his journey to another land was voluntary. Ramanujan's poetry explicates issues like heredity, ancestry, and roots which shall always remain relevant in diasporic literature.

In an overview on diaspora writings, Anjita Singh finds that the Indo-Anglian writers who have migrated abroad have been particularly fortunate in achieving awards and international acclaim due to their being diasporic. However, she is of the opinion that expatriation leads to lack of empathy with their native land. Rushdie, Naipaul, Bharati Mukherjee, to name a few, reel under the pressure of "pleasing the West." This, according to her, is "a renunciation of allegiance." However, she sums up her essay by arriving at a conclusion that writers of Indian diaspora are actually doing justice to both their own country and the foreign land which is ultimately leading to "self-recognition" and "self-definition."

Deepak Upadhyay takes up a study of Naipaul's *An Area of Darkness* to research whether the Nobel Prize winner's repelling and revulsive notions about India are due to his own bias or are purely imaginative. For Naipaul, India is a land where darkness prevails and to escape the harsh realities of the land of his ancestors he needs to cover himself with darkness. For him, his experience of India was shattering, juxtaposed with land of his imagination, his memories of his ancestors and their resplendent culture. This creates in him a complete alienation, which coupled with his incapacity of a sense of belongingness and his Western upbringing, results in not being able to associate himself with the country and rises above the darkness that intervenes between him and India.

Jaya Kapoor's extensive research on the poetry of Agha Shahid Ali reveals Kashmiri culture and mythology. What is notable is his broad and secular perspective, which according to him, has given a distinct identity to Kashmir. The blend of Hindu and Muslim cultures of the past in Kashmir was a subject of Ali's poetry which also reflects his mental agony at the political upheaval in the land. This was also eroding the distinct Kashmiri culture and the life of the beautiful valley. His love for this land and his empathy with both sects helped him in mitigating the dominance of India and Pakistan on the Kashmir problem.

V.S. Naipaul's *A House for Mr. Biswas* is a "treatise on the pangs of exile" opines Sunita Rai in her research paper. She finds that the "House" is symbolic of emancipation from tyranny and oppression, and expresses the protagonist's sense of alienation, exile, and his struggle for identity. Naipaul has explicitly elaborated the plight of indentured labourers of India and their travails in Trinidad in his novel. The diasporic concerns are most pronounced in the book.

In his paper on Naipaul, Sanjay Swarnkar discusses the connotations of the term "diaspora" arriving at a conclusion that the assortment and variety of cultures, races, creeds, and religions initiated diasporic literature in the world in the twentieth century. He considers Naipaul to be "a beautiful flower of the diaspora" as V.S. Naipaul's exposure to varied cultures elevates him to transcend all boundaries of nations, religions, and races. His writings depict the amalgamation of three identities within him though he could not connect himself to any nationality, religion, or culture. His diasporic sensibilities have been elucidated marvellously in his novels on India.

Sudhir Kumar Arora's interpretation of the most often used term "diaspora" is the sense of alienation due to nostalgia. He makes a beautiful comparison of the "diasporic human" to an Indian bride who leaves her parents' abode and adapts herself to the alien environment of her in-laws' home. It is this notion and experience of homelessness, uprootedness, displacement, and alienation which find expression in Vikram Seth's poem "Homeless" which Sudhir Arora has taken up for study. Vikram Seth's quest for identity, stability, and peace within and outside is what the poet yearns for. In another poem "Unclaimed", Sudhir Arora discerns that Vikram Seth questions and condemns the social sanctity of marriage for it hinders the freedom. The diasporic sensibility lies in the title "Unclaimed" as the reader instantly thinks of the claimed or native land. Seth suffers from a sense of alienation and his inability to communicate with the known or claimed. This inability goads him to establish a physical relationship with a stranger. Sudhir Arora compares him to a crane fluttering in a cage, expressed by C.L. Khatri in his poem "A Crane in a Cage."

Analyzing diasporic consciousness and tracing its importance as a post-colonial feature, Gourhari Behera opines that internal displacement from one province to another also has its diasporic problems. Alka Sarogi's novel *Kalikatha: Via Bypass*, which the writer has discussed, indicates the consciousness and feeling of exile rampant in the Marwari community settled in Culcutta. Marwaris being a migratory community have always suffered and confronted issues of belongingness and identity. Alka Sarogi talks of the conduct and the "gaze" of the "host" city which gives rise to fear, uncertainity, and alienation. The novel is thus replete with diasporic concerns.

Jhumpa Lahiri's *The Namesake* delineates the struggle of a Bengali couple to adopt and adapt themselves to the culture and social set-up of New York city. Jaba Kusum Singh senses the diasporic sensitivity in the very first sentence of the novel. Ashima clings to her own culture by preserving and following Bengali traditions. She is unable to accept America as her home. However, Jhumpa Lahiri shows that the second generation ladies, Ashima's daughter Sonia and her daughter-in-law Meenakshi, easily adopt the global culture. Jaba Kusum Singh's research on the novel finds the celebration of the beginning of a cosmopolitan culture that is comfortable and accepts all international customs and traditions. Lahiri suggests that to be at home in an alien country is to be multicultural and openly welcome as well as integrate new values.

P.K. Singh critically analyzes the diasporic characteristics in Bharati Mukherjee's *Jasmine*. Like her heroine, Bharati Mukherjee too faces the dilemma of an immigrant. The autobiographical element runs throughout the novel. P.K. Singh observes that the novelist believes that to acclimatize onself to a foreign culture in a foreign land is important to forget one's past life. Through her ever-changing identities, geographical locations and social milieu, Jasmine emerges as a strong woman eager to accept American culture and be a part of it. This happens due to her appreciating the American work culture and their freedom of thinking.

Prakash Chandra Pradhan discusses diasporic identity in V.S. Naipaul's *Half a Life* and *Magic Seeds*. The post-imperialistic situations of individuals who are constantly displaced from their original stands and identities when the values and socio-political realities keep on changing rapidly, depicted by Naipaul, have been ably brought out in the article.

Awanish Rai presents an interesting and inculcating comparison between old and new diaspora. Ashutosh Singh analyzes the issue of diaspora from the perspective of the Indian immigrants' struggle to maintain their identity. He takes up

Jhumpa Lahiri's novel, *Unaccustomed Earth* as the focus of his study.

Namrata Rathore Mahanta deals with the points of departure between the India projected in V.S. Naipaul's *An Area of Darkness* and the India of Naupaul's critics. Mahanta also brings references from Nissim Ezekiel's essay, "Naipaul's India and Mine" to establish that alongside all the squalor and poverty, there is enough positive in modern India.

Amod Kumar Rai shows how Kiran Desai's *The Inheritance of Loss* explores colonial neurosis, bitter experiences, insurgency, racial discrimination, etc. as well as the consequences of the introduction of western elements into Indian society.

The book will be useful for the students of Indian English literature and researchers in India diasporic writing.

R.P. Pradhan
Supriya Shukla

Contents

Preface ... *v*

List of Contributors ... *xiii*

1. A.K. Ramanujan: Journey Towards Roots ... 1
Shiv Govind Puri

2. Diaspora: A Renunciation of Allegiance? ... 7
Anjita Singh

3. The Coloured Darkness: A Study of Naipaul's *An Area of Darkness* ... 17
Deepak Upadhyay

4. Kashmir Across Ages and Beyond Conflicts in the Poetry of Agha Shahid Ali ... 27
Jaya Kapoor

5. V.S. Naipaul as a Diasporic Writer with Special Reference to *A House for Mr. Biswas* ... 38
Sunita Rai

6. V.S. Naipaul's Concept of Diaspora ... 47
Sanjay Swarnkar

7. Vikram Seth's "Homeless" and "Unclaimed": A View through the Diasporic Lenses ... 53
Sudhir K. Arora

8. Mapping the Trajectory of Internal Migration: Alka Saraogi's *Kalikatha: Via Bypass* 64
Gourhari Behera

9. Jhumpa Lahiri's *The Namesake*: A Tale of Diasporic Consciousness 70
Jaba Kusum Singh

10. Diasporic Sensibility in Bharati Mukherjee's *Jasmine* 79
P.K. Singh

11. Situating Diasporic Identity in V.S. Naipaul's *Half a Life* and *Magic Seeds* 90
Prakash Chandra Pradhan

12. Indian Diaspora: Old and New 135
Awanish Rai

13. Meteoric Identity and Transcultural Experiences of Indian Diaspora in Jhumpa Lahiri's *Unaccustomed Earth* 145
Ashutosh Singh

14. India of the Mind: Homeland and Diasporic Contingencies... 168
Namrata Rathore Mahanta

15. Contamination Perpetrated by Diaspora 175
Amod Kumar Rai

List of Contributors

Shiv Govind Puri. Associate Professor, Dept. of English and MEL, University of Lucknow, Uttar Pradesh.

Anjita Singh. Associate Prof. in English, A.N.D.N.N.M.M., Kanpur, Uttar Pradesh.

Deepak Upadhyay. Associate Professor, Dept. of English, Agra College, Agra, Uttar Pradesh.

Jaya Kapoor. Associate Professor, Dept. of English and M.E.L. University of Allahabad, Uttar Pradesh.

Sunita Rai. Assistant Professor, K.N.P.S.S. Sultanpur, Uttar Pradesh.

Sanjay Swarnkar. Associate Professor, Dept. of English, CSJM University, Kanpur, Uttar Pradesh.

Sudhir K. Arora. Associate Professor, Department of English, Maharaja Harishchandra P.G. College, Moradabad, Uttar Pradesh.

Gourhari Behera. Associate Professor, Department of English, DDU Gorakhpur University, Gorakhpur, Uttar Pradesh.

Jaba Kusum Singh. Assistant Professor, Dept. of English, Upadhi P.G. College, Pilibhit, Uttar Pradesh.

P.K. Singh. Associate Professor & Head Dept. of English, Sakaldiha P.G. College, Sakaldiha, Chandauli, Uttar Pradesh.

Prakash Chandra Pradhan. Professor, Dept. of English, BHU, Varanasi.

Awanish Rai. Associate Professor, Dept. of English, DDU Gorakhpur University, Gorakhpur.

Ashutosh Singh. Assistant Professor, Dept. of English, Guru Ghasidas Vishwavidyalaya (a Central University) Bilaspur, Chhatisgarh.

Namrata Rathore Mahanta. Associate Professor, Dept. of English, Mahila Mahavidyalaya, BHU, Varanasi.

Amod Kumar Rai. Assistant Professor, Dept. of English, BPG college, Kushinagar (U.P.)

1

A.K. Ramanujan: Journey Towards Roots

Shiv Govind Puri

Ramanujan's poetry in English marks a very important strand—that of the diasporic Indian in relation to his motherland, and he happens to be one of the earliest diasporic writers from India. 'Diaspora' is a mechanical term which was first time used in the Old Testament of the Bible under the Line no. 25: "Thou shall be a diaspora in all the kingdoms of the earth" later on used by the writers with all those people who move from one place to the other. This term was frequently used by the writers from time to time without concerning the whole idea of using this term, written in the background. It became a matter of fashion and commerce in literature. Therefore, the critic and scholar, Makarand Paranjpe suggested two of the perspectives on which this term may be confined, i.e. transnational and transcultural aspects. Now this vision has been a part of diaspora across the culture and discipline. Diaspora is a metaphorical term, and there are three different metaphorical constructions of it, one is the metaphor of imaginary homelands created by immigrant writers such as Salman Rushdie. The second part is of the space shared by those who are part of diaspora which reflects in the part of literature and history of their land. Third is the metaphor of the journey as an intrinsic part of diaspora itself. So, the third part of diaspora 'searching towards roots' is related to Ramanujan and his nostalgic experiences. Interestingly, however, his poems do not always tell us a story, the narrative is not very clear all the time, we need to figure out from the metaphors and the symbols what it is signifying. Now, I quote a few lines from his poem, "Conventions of Despair":

> Of ideal Tomorrow's Crowfoot eyes
> And the theory of a peacock Feathered future.
> No, no, give me back my Archaic despair:
> it's not obsolete yet to live
> In this many-Lived lair (13)

A.K. Ramanujan defends himself when he was said as a person of expatriate culture and identity, thus:

> No, an exile is a person who has been thrown out of his country I'm not one. I have come to this country voluntarily.... I don't call myself an expatriate, because I've done a lot of work on India since coming to this country. I've done it more comfortably here than I could even have done it in India.... And the other interesting thing is that one can be an Internal alien in India, as one goes from one province to another. I have lived in my own language, region since my 20th year. If you go a hundred miles away, you are in a language that you cannot read or speak.... I think it is in the dialogue of three cultures, which I sometimes refer to as downstairs, upstairs and outside the house—and in the between these three languages, that, I am made. (Keith Taylor 52-53)

As a postcolonial poet, Ramanujan is singularly unique. He combines in him the vision of folklorist, the vision of a poet, and the skill of a translator. Though he is at once an expatriate and a postcolonial poet, he successfully turns the expatriate condition and the postcolonial situation to his advantage and brings the image of India and the implicit culture of the country alive in his poetry. In the poem, "Extended Family", the poet seeks to examine and compare his self with the so-called modern culture of America. This is a kind of nostalgic viewpoint which comes here and there in his poems. The poet discovers, the naked bathing speaker to present the self in relation to others:

> Yet like grandfather
> I bathe before the village crow

The dry chlorine water
My only Ganges
The naked Chicago bulb
A cousin of the Vedic sun. (169)

The poet tries to portray his viewpoint through the poem, as a member of an "Extended Family" living simultaneously in different cultures and writing about them. In his poems, I find a desperate effort to relate more meaningfully to the cultural sites that are no longer available to him as a diasporic person, there is certainly no battle, but the tension of trying to analyze one's relationship to the past broods over his poems and the family returns as the topic again and again. Ramanujan's characteristics to his past emerges his peculiar relationship to it, he tries to think about the past with a nostalgia that betrays his deep anchor in it. He repeatedly speaks of his family, the places and the events in an India that he no longer lives in it, his poems tell us how much his present is trapped in a past that holds so much meaning for him. In "Conventions of Despair", Ramanujan accepts the truth that something has not been achieved in his life. That is the quest for his identity so he regrets:

conventions of despair
they have their pride
I must seek and will find
my particular hell only in
my Hindu mind:
must translate and turn
till I blister and roast. (12)

There is the feeling of loss and unattainable love to his country. That attachment and dislocation from the native soil visualises the social milieu of Indian ethos. Ramanujan's longings and attachment to the native land cannot be constricted to the culture only. Ramanujan once wrote:

> English and my disciplines (Linguistics, anthropology) give me my 'outer' forms—linguistic, metrical, logical and other such ways of shaping experience; and my first thirty years in India, my frequent visits and fieldtrips, my personal and professional preoccupations with Kannada,

> Tamil, the Classics and Folklore give me my substance my 'inner' forms, images and symbols. They are continuous with each other, and I no longer can tell what comes from where. (Parthasarathy 96)

In the light of Ramanujan's diasporic perspective, let us attempt an analysis of his poetry where Hindu legends and mythological stories prove his integration with Indian cultural past. Ramanujan's four poetical collections of poetry—"The Striders" (1966), "Relations: Poems" (1971), "Second Sight" (1986), and "The Black Hen" (1995) bears out this truth. In the first volume, we have a poem like "Snakes" where the ritual of worshipping snakes (nagas) on the Nagpanchami day in the month of shravan is remarkably highlighted. It is a ritual which is still practised in our villages and towns with a good deal of zeal and zest. The second volume unfolds the legend of burning Kamdeva by Lord Shiva. Ramanujan's myths appear every now and then in his poems as a part of poetic strategy in a given context. It was the poet's poetic sensibility to touch the core of human heart,

> The breast she offered was
> Full of poison and milk.
> Flashing eyes suddenly dull,
> Her voice was silk. (79)

Therefore in this poem, Baby Krishna sucks not only the poisonous milk but her life too. Paradoxically having been killed by God, she, redeemed of all her sins, attains salvation.

Apart from mythological expressions, Ramanujan's historic sensibility is sharp and acute. The linking of the familial experience with the historical consciousness is a feature which runs through the poetry of Ramanujan from an early poem like "Conventions of Despair" to the last poem in "Relations" the pathetic one "Prayers to Lord Murugan" with an intrinsic vision, Ramanujan evokes the recurring pattern of historical tragedy and individual suffering. His poems appear with the anxiety of the individual and the anxiety of the people long subjected to misery and thraldom. Ramanujan portrays the nostalgia of collective people who look back, often in an attitude of love-hate, to the past, at once drawn towards and repelled by it. In the poem, "History", Ramanujan expresses his longings with the native land,

> which usually changes slowly.
> changes sometimes during a single conversation:
> the petite little aunt
> in her garden of sweet limes
> Now carries a different
> Face, not merely older or colder
> Or made holy
> By deaths and children's failures. (47)

The awareness and assurance of rootedness establishes emotional stability and enables him to integrate the past and present, the immediate and the remote, all that is within and without, the Western work-orientedness and the Indian human relationship. In "Second Sight", Ramanujan's fascination comes forth for issues such as heredity, ancestry and roots. The metaphor of the diaspora, 'journey towards roots' certainly extend and empower the cultural and aesthetic values of immigration, hybridity and diaspora-ization. The poem shows that the springs of Ramanujan's creativity continue to be in his Indian roots, and an art rooted in the soil will always remain vital. The title poem, "Second Sight" itself illustrates. Thus, speaker here tells us that:

> In Pascal's endless queue
> ...As we enter the dark
> Somconc says from bchind
> "You're a Hindu, aren't you?
> Must have second sight.
>
> (Naik, *History of Indian English Literaure* 149)

This poem just offers the poet's fascination towards the Indian view of life.

To conclude, Ramanujan's diasporic experiences are very different from any other writers of the time. As Avtar Brah argues that home remains a mythical place of desire in the imagination and a place of no return for the diasporic writers. Ramanujan transforms this myth into a realized experience by passionately clinging to and constructing such rare images of home and family authenticate his identity. In "Returning", he creates such an ethos:

> Returning home one blazing afternoon
> He looked for his mother every where
> She was not in the kitchen,
> She wasn't in the backyard she wasn't any where
> Where are you? I'm home! I'm hungry
> But there was no answer, not even an echo
> In the deserted street blazing with sunshine.
> Suddenly he remembered he was now sixty-one
> And he hadn't had a mother for forty years.
> (*Uncollected Poems* 4)

Ramanujan has multiple layers of 'identity' in which certain things do not go away, do not disappear despite physical displacement or geographical dislocation from his poetry. Ramanujan's views are still relevant today when we are approaching towards the multicultural forces of identity where people have reached to change the worldview. We have travelled from "Desperate Diaspora" to "Dollar Diaspora". Now moving out of the people from one land to another land has been become a matter of fashion, a matter of recognition which is not the background of old diaspora. I think this is the gradual development of need and the purpose of life. Ramanujan's view of nostalgic experiences can be viewed under the canon of old diaspora.

Works Cited

Naik, M.K. *Indian English Literature (1980-2000).* Delhi: Pencraft, 2001. Print.

Quoted in R. Parthasarathy. Ed. *Ten Twentieth Century Indian Poets.* New Delhi: Oxford University Press, 2004. Print.

Ramanujan, A.K. *The Collected Poems.* New Delhi: Oxford University Press, 1995. Print.

Ramanujan, A.K., A.L. Becker and Keith Taylor. "Interview Two". *Uncollected Poems and Prose.* Ed. Molly Daniels. Delhi: University Press, 2001. Print.

Upadhyay, O.N. *Perspectives on Indian Diaspora.* New Delhi: Sarup Book Publishers, 2014. Print.

2

Diaspora: A Renunciation of Allegiance?

Anjita Singh

The term "diaspora" in addition to its original meaning of a scattering of population basically pertains to a community in exile from its native land involuntarily or otherwise. Expatriation is the term that comes closest to being a synonym and naturally involves the idea of a homeland from which the displacement or expatriation has occurred. An interesting observation about expatriation and its accompanied dilemma has been made by Jaiwanti Dimri (though the context was slightly different as she is referring to second generation immigrants whose sentiments definitely vary from those of the first generation expatriates). Dimri describes the expatriate experience as "problematic" for the reason that voluntary immigrants are "free from the stigma of nostalgia and any symptoms of angst loneliness or existential rootlessness and homelessness" (28), because to them, expatriation is only an imaginary reality. Co-incidentally, in the legal sense expatriation also means a renunciation of allegiance. The suggestion that arises is if diaspora is equivalent to expatriation and expatriation leads to gradual but definite renunciation of allegiance then the diaspora is a group of people who due to various reasons or compulsions come to live in a different country and acknowledge not much empathy with the country of their birth or ancestry. And if they do not allow fancy, the obligation of that identity labelling them with the tag of the homeland is absurd and unrequired. It is generally argued that because the term diaspora carries a sense of displacement and the population so described finds itself for whatever reason separated from its national territory, its people would have a hope, or at least a desire, to return to their homeland at some point. However, some writers have noted that diaspora may result in a loss of nostalgia for a single home as people re-root in a series of displacements (the most apt example is of Sir Vidiyadhar Surajprasad himself). Displacement is a calamity in many ways yet, the curiously paradoxical observation is that the changed atmosphere seems to provide a stronger stimulant propelling writers in their displaced existence to have a tendency to excel in their work. In an interview with Nikhil Padgaonkar for Doordarshan, Edward W. Said reflecting on the condition of expatriation says:

> I think that if one is an intellectual, one has to exile oneself from what has been given to you, what is customary, and to see it from a point of view that looks at it as if it were something that is provisional and foreign to oneself. That allows for independence and a certain kind of detachment. (13)

Rushdie reiterates the same sentiment when he says that "to migrate is to experience deep change and wrenches in the soul" and that "the migrant is not simply transformed by his act, he also transforms the new world". Migrants do undergo the process of mutation but such hybridization leads to the emergence of newness.

In both his works *Midnight's Children* and *Imaginary Homelands,* Rushdie is searching for his identity both as person whose roots are in India and as a writer who wants to establish himself among British writers. It is this complexity of situation which encourages in him a new level of maturity and innovation.

The Indian diaspora has been formed by a scattering of population and not, in the Jewish sense, an exodus of population at a particular point in time. This sporadic migration traces a steady pattern over a period of time: from the indentured labourers of the past to the IT technocrats of the present day. Sudesh Mishra divides the Indian diaspora into two categories—

the old and the new. He writes that, "This distinction is between, on the one hand, the semi-voluntary flight of indentured peasants to non-metropolitan plantation colonies such as Fiji, Trinidad, Mauritius, South Africa, Malaysia, Surinam, and Guyana, roughly between the years 1830 and 1917; and the other the late capital or postmodern dispersal of new migrants of all classes to thriving metropolitan centres such as Australia, the United States, Canada, and Britain" (276). The Indian diasporic community has acquired a new identity due to the processes of adaptation and increasing acceptance by the West especially after Independence. The history of diasporic Indian writing is as old as the diaspora itself. By exemplifying writers both from the old Indian diaspora of indentured labourers and the modern Indian diaspora of IT technocrats, it shows that despite peculiarities there is an inherent exilic state in all dislocated lives whether it be voluntary or involuntary migration. Diasporic Indian writing is in this sense also a part of exile literature. More importantly, a broad survey of the contributions of the second generation of the modern Indian diaspora in the field of Indian writing in English depicts certain shift in concerns in comparison to the previous generation and thereby it widens the perspective of exile literature.

The Indo-Anglian literary scene reveals a rather extraordinary and startling fact. It is intriguing that in the sphere of literary success (if success translates to having global recognition through acceptance by international publishing houses, and being nominated for prestigious literary awards such as the Booker or Pulitzer) luck is partial to those writers (of Indian descent) who are famously known as the members of the diaspora. On a survey the names that emerge most eminently are of those such as, V.S. Naipaul, Salman Rushdie, Amitav Ghosh, Bharati Mukherjee, Rohinton Mistri, Jhumpa Lahiri, Kiran Desai, Neel Mukherjee. The common thread between them all is that they all belong to the haloed-glorified group called the diaspora. These are the writers who have been nominated for or have won international prizes and who are believed to represent the best of India. But the perplexing implication is that expatriation is the necessary condition for literary identification. Rukun Advani in his essay, "Novelists in Residence", argued that the rising Indo-Anglian novel was inextricably tied to the rising Indian middle-classes, and that most significant new Indo-Anglian novelists had passed through the holy triumvirate of Doon School (India's most elite boys' only public school), the super-privileged St Stephen's College (in Advani's words, "an unusually attractive blend of Cambridge and the redder bricks of Delhi") and then, either Oxford or Cambridge. These thrice-blessed writers whom Advani named 'the Ghosh generation' (after Amitav Ghosh), all, allegedly, emerged out of a fertile and hybridised cultural soil. Amit Chaudhuri very pertinently questions—"Can it be true that Indian writing, that endlessly rich, complex and problematic entity, is to be represented by a handful of writers who write in English, who live in England or America and whom one might have met at a party?" It is ironical that the Indian soil which can germinate the embryo lacks the environment to bring it to fruition. Evidently, the writers earning a name for themselves internationally are all members of that group identified as the diaspora but who in rather straight words have abandoned the homeland (read India) for greener pastures (read the West).

The employing of magical realism, bagginess, non-linear narrative and hybrid language in Indian Writing in English (IWE for short) to sustain themes seen as microcosms of India and supposedly reflecting Indian conditions started after Independence and is a trend in contrast to the works of earlier writers such as Narayan where the use of English is wholesome. Indianness is a theme constructed only in IWE by this group and is not expressed in the vernacular literatures. Postcolonial theory points to these kinds of postures adopted by writers labouring under the pressure of pleasing the West. The views of Salman Rushdie and Amit Chaudhuri expressed through their books *The Vintage Book of Indian Writing* and *The Picador Book of Modern Indian Literature*, respectively draw attention to this clash. Chaudhuri writes, "the postcolonial novel becomes a trope for an ideal hybridity by which the West celebrates not so much Indianness, whatever that infinitely complex thing is, but its own historical quest, its reinterpretation of itself". It is Said's claim, specifically in his monumental *Culture and Imperialism* (1993), that the nineteenth-century novel was principally a cultural form which refined and articulated the political hegemony of Empire and, therefore, Englishness. The main thrust of Said's argument is that the nineteenth-century novel was the definitive cultural form through which the 'West' represented and narrated its possession of the rest. In order to successfully activate the different practices, it became necessary to be a certain sort of cosmopolitan individual, educated and employable in the 'West', mobile, migratory, diasporic. To put this simply: so as to always speak back to the West, it is crucial to speak in a way that the West understands, publishes and, paradoxically, authorises.

Consequently, it would not be entirely erroneous to say that these expatriate writers feel a renunciation of allegiance towards the land of their ancestry. As one of Naipaul's characters in his *A Bend in the River* says "...home was hardly a place I could return to...home was something in my head. It was something I had lost". Naipaul's fictional and non-fictional writings respond to the need to discover an appropriate literary form to frame the psychic and symbolic sense of 'homelessness'. The account of his expatriate experience reveals the pain of his displacement, though at the same time it makes him cynical about other races and cultures including that of India. V.S. Naipaul born in Trinidad in 1932 the descendent of indentured labourers shipped from India is the true dispossessed son of the Raj. For Naipaul the possibility to return home never existed. He was disengaged physically as well as emotionally from his homeland.

The modern diasporic Indian writers too can be grouped into two distinct categories. One comprises those who have spent a part of their life in India and have carried the baggage of their native land offshore. The other class comprises those who have been bred since childhood outside India. They have had a view of their country only from the outside as an exotic place of their origin. The writers of the former group have a literal displacement whereas those belonging to the latter group find themselves rootless. Both the groups of writers have produced an enviable corpus of English literature. These writers while depicting migrant characters in their fiction explore the theme of displacement and self-fashioning. The diasporic Indian writers' depiction of dislocated characters gains greater realism when seen against the geo-political background of the vast Indian subcontinent.

Immigration is not a very attractive experience to the diaspora; it is understandably traumatic owing to the clash of two cultures and the racial discrimination that is predictably involved. Immigration proves a pleasant experience only to those who succeed in assimilating themselves with the new geographical, cultural, social and psychological environment. Makarand Paranjape notes "that instead of worshipping the leftovers and relics of now inaccessible homeland, as the old diaspora of indentured labourers did, the new diaspora of international Indian English writers live close to their market, in the comforts of the suburbia of advanced capital but draw their raw material from the inexhaustible imaginative resources of that messy and disorderly subcontinent that is India" (252). These writers record their way from India experiences and even if they look back at their homeland, it is often in an elegiac tone rather than with nostalgia. Paranjape explicates this point in considering the novels of Rohinton Mistry. Ultimately, Indian writers in the West are increasingly identifying themselves with the literary tradition of the migrant writers of the world. Rushdie says that "Swift, Conrad, Marx [and even Melville, Hemingway, Bellow] are as much our literary forebears as Tagore or Ram Mohan Roy" (20).

Bharati Mukherjee has gone on record to say that she considers herself an American writer, and not an Indian expatriate writer. In an 1989 interview with Amanda Meer, Mukherjee said:

> I totally consider myself an American writer, and that has been my big battle: to get to realize that my roots as a writer are no longer, if they ever were, among Indian writers, but that I am writing about the territory, about the feelings, of a new kind of pioneer here in America. I'm the first among Asian immigrants to be making this distinction between immigrant writing and expatriate writing. Most

> Indian writers prior to this, have still thought of themselves as Indians, and their literary inspiration, has come from India. India has been the source, and home. Whereas I'm saying, those are wonderful roots, but now my roots are here and my emotions are here in North America. While Mukherjee has been received favorably by many critics and academics, she has also faced a good deal of criticism, particularly from East Indian scholars and critics. It has been said that she often represents India in her fiction as a land without hope or a future.

Mukherjee has established herself as a powerful member of the American literary scene, one whose most memorable works reflect her pride in her Indian heritage, but also and more, her celebration of embracing America.

In the words of Salman Rushdie, "home has become a scattered, damaged, various concept" and this condition of "living here and belonging elsewhere" has affected people in an unprecedented fashion. The narrator of *The Ground Beneath Her Feet* gives a positive turn to this kind of mobility believing that "in every generation, blessed or cursed, there are a few souls that are born not belonging...". These people come into the world semi-detached...'without strong affiliation to family or location or nation or race'. Recalling the famous opening of L.P. Hartley's novel *The Go-Between*, that reads "the past is a foreign country—they do things differently there", Rushdie inverts the idea when he looks at an old photograph: "it reminds me that it's my present that is foreign, and that the past is home, albeit a lost home in a lost city in the mists of lost time" (9). He sees himself, in this respect, as one who writes from outside India trying to reflect that lost world and in doing so he is dealing with "broken mirrors" (11), never with the complete and actual reality. This image of the "broken mirrors" is very compelling because of its fragmentary condition. Diasporic migrants are necessarily fragmented, as they have been dispersed and torn away from their country and fellow citizens. So, like memory, which is faulty and partial and may thus lead into distortions and falsifications of history, the diasporic writer is faced with the challenge of remembering and rewriting the past left behind.

Fragmentation, which initially might be seen as a weakness, thus turns into strength, allowing the writer to imagine his past, giving him more freedom to create and to recover the lost time, the lost home. It could even be said that writers like Rushdie, experiencing this sort of diaspora in Britain, feel empowered by precisely the tradition of immigration and diasporas of the past. He puts it very clearly when he reclaims for his own art and writing the traditions that Britain has incorporated throughout its history:

> Let me suggest that Indian writers in England have access to a second tradition, quite apart from their own racial history. It is the culture and political history of the phenomenon of migration, displacement, life in a minority group. We can quite legitimately claim as our ancestors the Huguenots, the Irish, the Jews; the past to which we belong is an English past, the history of immigrant Britain. (20)

Amitav Ghosh is perhaps the first Indian author who aptly describes the uprooted native's dilemma in an alien context through thematic interpretation. He avoids being pulled into the quagmire of the status quo of diasporic literature and allows modern Western aesthetics to influence his writing freely. In his refusal to accept the Eurasian Commonwealth Writers Prize for his book *The Glass Palace*, he tries to prove his intention in a letter written to the administrators of the Commonwealth Prize in March 2001

> I have on many occasions publicly stated my objections to the classification of books such as mine under the term "commonwealth literature". Principal among these is that this phrase anchors an area of contemporary writing not within the realities of the present day, nor within the possibilities of the future, but rather within a disputed aspect of the past....

Ghosh here is speaking in the same vein as Gayatri Spivak in essence denying the position he is attributed with by the literary-cultural scenario. Similarly, Jhumpa Lahiri, Pulitzer Prize winner, born in London to Indian immigrants who finally moved to and settled down in the United States is a writer uncomfortable under the label of IWE. Lahiri considers herself truly American, stating, "I wasn't born here but I might as well have been" and yet her writing addresses sensitive dilemmas in the lives of Indian immigrants.

Diasporic cultural development assumes a different course from that of the population in the original place of settlement. Over time, remotely separated communities tend to vary in culture, traditions, language and other factors and accordingly the responses of the diasporic writers to India are also varied. Not always adulatory, they range from sentimentality and nostalgia to a cynical celebration of their coming of age. However, their diasporic condition, their sense of exile and alienation and their efforts to seek replenishment by making symbolic returns to their origins bind all this writing into a unity. Writers of the Indian Diaspora have been at the centre stage chiefly because of the theoretical formulation generated by their works. Living on the margins of two countries and cultures these writers attempt to do justice to both. Diaspora may be described as a journey towards self-recognition and self-definition. The unmistakable element of creativity in their writings stands as a compensation for the many losses suffered.

Works Cited

Advani, Rukun. "Novelists in Residence". *The Fiction of St. Stephen's*. Eds. A. Bhattacharjea and L. Chatterjee. New Delhi: Ravi Dayal, 2000. Print.

Chaudhuri, Amit (Ed.). *The Picador Book of Modern Indian Literature*. London: Picador, 2001. Print.

Dimri, Jaiwanti. "Feminist Discourse on Expatriation: A Study of Ravinder Randhawa's *A Wicked Old Woman* and Atima Srivastava's *Transmission*". *Literary Voice Book Series*, 5 Feb. 2000. Print.

Mishra, Sudesh. "From Sugar to Masala: Writing by the Indian Diaspora". *An Illustrated History of Indian Literature in English*. Ed. Arvind Krishna Mehrotra. New Delhi: Permanent Black, 2003. Print.

Paranjpe, Makarand. "Triple Ambivalence; Australia, Canada and South Asia in the Diasporic Imagination". *Journal of Department of English*, Vol. XXXII. Calcutta University. 2005-06. Print.

Rushdie, Salman. "Imaginary Homelands". *Essays and Criticism, 1981-1991*. London: Granta Books in association with Penguin Books. Print.

Saha, Amit. "Exile Literature and the Diasporic Indian Writer". *Rupkatha Journal on Interdisciplinary Studies in Humanities*. Vol. I, No. 2, Autumn 2009. Print.

Said, Edward W. "Reflections of an Exile". *A Review of Books*, Vol. IV, Numbers 11 and 12. Ed. Arvind N. Das. New Delhi: Brinda Datta, Nov.-Dec. 1999. Print.

———. *Culture and Imperialism*. New York: Alfred A. Knopf, 1993. Print.

3

The Coloured Darkness: A Study of Naipaul's *An Area of Darkness*

Deepak Upadhyay

For the coveted Nobel Prize that was earmarked in literature for 'outstanding work of idealistic tendency', Naipaul appeared to many of us as the most "ironic and controversial choice".[1] His brutal and ruthless observations on the postcolonial world, and more particularly on the Indian subcontinent, drew for him immense hostilities and anger. He invited much controversy for his politically incorrect views of the "half made societies". Edward Said argues that "Naipaul allowed himself quite consciously to be turned into a witness for the western prosecution", promoting what Said classifies as, "colonial mythologies about wogs and darkies". Critic like C.D. Narsimhaiah opines that Naipaul has "profaned the exalted vocation of the writer, and he has set for himself the goal of being before the public constantly by generating controversy after controversy".[2] He further believes that Naipaul denigrated human beings whereas an artist should try to add dignity to humanity. Naipaul was accused of looking at India through Western kaleidoscope which takes myriad unreal shapes when aimed at lighted areas. On the contrary, the Swedish Academy while awarding him the Nobel Prize, noted his insistence on writing about "peripheral people" with "having united perceptive narrative and incorruptible scrutiny in works that compel us to see the presence of the suppressed histories". It further appreciates Naipaul for dealing extensively with shifting identities, roots, homes and the changing realities of the migrants. In the light of the above contentious issues and views, this short paper is a modest attempt "to look and to look again, to relook and to rethink" about Naipaul's inquiries into the complexities of the pluralistic ideologies of Indian Nation. It will try to unravel the truth of his accusation of India as a world of "myth and darkness", and "chaos and confusion". It will also explore whether his contemplation of India as dark, dirty, diseased and corrupt have even an ounce of truth or they are merely Naipaul's figments of imagination and prejudice.

In one of his articles, Prof. Narasimhaiah refers to his meeting with Naipaul who was well aware of the writer's ire and, therefore, tries to mollify him by saying that he is "profoundly Indian in his feeling, and profoundly Indian in his sensibility, but not in his observation".[3] Prof. Narasimhaiah raises his objection and says mere 'observation' is insufficient for a writer; he must have his own conviction and emotion and faith and belief as well. This conflict is nothing but the result of the difference of the perception and attitude wherein Narasimhaiah follows Matthew Arnold and T.S. Eliot who laid emphasis on the traditional values, and Naipaul on the dissenting individual talent, emphatic of a subjective self that experiences reality and passes judgement accordingly. The India that existed in an area of the imagination in Naipaul's mind is shattered in the very first encounter itself. The first trip, the fruit being of which *An Area of Darkness,* happens to be much traumatic and harrowing. The childhood faith in his ancestral 'home' is dispelled by Naipaul's first encounter with its dust and dirt, and poverty and corruption, and there emerges his love-hate relationship with India resulting in a painful realization of irresolvable estrangement, and he says, "I came of a family that abounded with pundits. But I had been born an unbeliever" (32). For such an agonistic mind, corruption and squalor would have certainly prejudiced him against the brighter side of India. India's poverty continues to draw his attention throughout the book, and he remarks, "I had seen the starved children defecating at the roadside while the mangy dog waited to eat the excrement" (45). What distresses him further in this context is that it is not only a village scene in India, but it is frequently visible in every part of the country, be it on the slopes of Kashmir or on the beaches of Goa. He, sometimes, passes sarcastic remarks when he says, "not all the sandal oil perfumes of Lucknow could hide the stench of gutters and latrines" (46). "Sometimes, he gets humorous at places and says that defecating is a social activity; they squat close to one another, they chatter" (70). Even more he is amused to find a spiritual element attached to this social act. Owing to Indians' love for nature, they prefer to wake up early in the morning, and rush towards the river and ease themselves out, "nothing was as poetic as squatting on a river bank at dawn". He refers to Mahatma Gandhi's idea of sanitation here, which, deplorably for him, Indians have completely ignored.

> Sanitation was linked to caste, caste to callousness, inefficiency and a hopelessly divided country, division to weakness, weakness to foreign rule. That is what Gandhi saw, and no one purely of India would have seen it. (74)

Naipaul is also aghast at the transformation of Gandhi only in Indian archives, and not being used as a living reference of guidance and inspiration. When Naipaul arrives in Delhi, he is affronted by the screeching and screaming porters at the railway station, whining beggars, scuttling auto-rickshaws outside, surrounded by "a jungle of black and white notice boards" (83). Obviously, his initial reaction about Delhi has been critical and he remarks, "It was as though an Indian village had been transformed into concrete and glass, and magnified" (85). But when he meets his hostess Mrs. Mahindra and her bubbling warmth and genuine concern for him, he seems to be little mollified and placated. Though he is a paying guest of Mrs. Mahindra, the behaviour of the landlady is all full of womanly care and "touched with genuine Indian warmth", and there seems no business in it at all (91). Despite the departure from Mrs. Mahindra's house, the reason being her husband's disapproval, his fondness for her seems unchanged and uninterrupted. Occasionally, there are some light-hearted comments on her character as she being crazy for anything forcign and wants to marry her son to a foreign girl. Nonetheless, it is here for the first time in the book that we see that Naipaul has something good to think of India.

Outside, Mrs. Mahindra's house, Delhi is almost as callous as Bombay, which makes Naipaul infuriated, depleted and at times disgraced at the official aloofness. He narrates, for instance, "Don't complain to me. Complain to my officer. Which is your bloody officer? All this with a liberating sense that my violent mood was inviting violence" (92). He sees the hangover of colonial days still apparent in Delhi in spite of the gusto of the newly emerging capital of Independent India. After the unbearable heat of Delhi, the next destination of Naipaul is Kashmir, and the writer is overwhelmed at the sensuous beauty of the surroundings: "Kashmir was coolness and colour: the yellow mustard field, the mountains, snow capped, milky blue sky in which we rediscovered the drama of clouds" (95). At Srinagar, he hires a room from Mr. M.S. Butt, the owner of hotel Liward, and stays there for many weeks. And there he is all the time surrounded by Aziz. After Mrs. Mahindra, this Aziz is another person who has been characterized with warmth and humane touch notwithstanding his constant penchant for bakshish and remorseless robbing of the author of a few dozen rupees. Naipaul brings Aziz to all the places of tourist attraction outside Srinagar. In this context, he gives graphic details of the celebrations of the Muslim holy month. He remarks: "Religion was a spectacle, and festivals, women veiled (so that men wouldn't get excited and think bad things, the merchant said), women bred and breeding like battery hens; it was the ceremonial washing of the genitals in public prayers: it was ten thousand simultaneous prostrations" (128).

Later, in order to gain some idea of Indian culture, Naipaul visits a writer's party at Srinagar where he is surprised to find out that artistic talent is equated with writer's melancholic and alcoholic disposition. He is puzzled to note that, "In India poets and musicians are required to live the part: It is necessary to be sad and alcoholic" (132-33). However, even in Kashmir, Naipaul is distraught by the prevalence of the cancerous corruption in political circles. The Indian Government was pouring millions of rupees in Kashmir, but to no avail. What pains him further is that no shame is coming to those corrupt people; instead, a lot of social prestige and status is bestowed on such unscrupulous officials:

> It is estimated that in Kashmir, as in the rest of India, one third of development funds drains away in corruption and the exchanging of gifts. No disgrace attaches to this (sic). The Kashmiri tailor spoke with admiration of his patwari friend, a surveyor and type of records keeper, who in one day might collect as much as a hundred rupees; a lorry driver had a similar admiration for traffic inspector he knew who received monthly protection money from various lorry drivers. (135)

Intermittently, there are cries against corruption in Parliament and on the other public forums also, but they are just token attempts to tide over public criticism. Eventually, the old system returns with intensified ferocity and ignominy. The writer, in this manner, has concluded that corruption has become deep-rooted in the Indian system of government and society. Sometimes, this system is as simple as inviting Mr. Madan of the tourist department by the writer to a tea party at the persistent request of Mr. Butt so that he can be issued a sort of permanent licence for his hotel. But most of the times, it is quite intricate and difficult to bypass.

While in Kashmir, Naipaul is encouraged by Karan Singh, the young Maharaja of Kashmir, to join the pilgrimage to the cave of Amarnath, the eternal abode of Lord Shiva. Although a non-believer, Naipaul joins the procession in order to have a first-hand feeling of religious India. He is deeply touched by the firm faith in religion: "The god existed: the faces and the cries of the returning pilgrims carried this reassurance. I wished I was of their spirit, I wished that something of their joy awaited me at the end" (167). On the contrary, instead of relishing religious fulfilment, Naipaul derives inexplicable joy of being among mountains, especially, the Himalayas. In his childhood fantasy of India, the Himalayas had a special place, a special claim. So travelling through those Himalayan peaks, full of meandering streams and enchanting greenery filled him with contentment of a unique dimension. Here again, the only disheartening experience for the writer is the horrible sanitation habits of the pilgrims and cheating by the pony owner. He is further surprised to know that Aziz is part of that fraudulence and has finally taken a few rupees from the pony owner as his commission.

By and large, *An Area of Darkness* is less the record of geographical travels and more that of journey inward, and the emotional sojourn of the author. Accordingly, he may further move to Shimla, Madras and Calcutta and there may be variations in topography, but his emotional attitude for the whole of India would be the same or rather further crystallized. In his visit to Shimla, what galls him further is the unabashed mimicry of colonial lifestyle of the people and the architecture all around. He wants to see India as India and not as further extension of the same old British Empire. As a result his confrontation with such an India is deeply disturbing: "It was an encounter with a humiliation I had never before experienced, and perhaps more so to me than those Indians who hurried about streets with unlikely English names, in the shadow of imperial grand house" (188). In addition, he is also vexed by the Indian attitude towards inheritance, Indian's obsession with preserving even those monuments which are the symbols of the Indian defeat, culturally or otherwise. For Naipaul most of these ruins and monuments are regressive and stumbling blocks for the progress of India: "...in India everything is inherited, nothing is abolished; everything grows out of something else...[piling] decay upon decay" (194).

In Madras, he finds the similar regressive tendency of looking back on the contemporary condition of the country through its past, which Naipaul concludes as "retreat into fantasy and fatalism" (201). What he expects from the Indians is to look directly upon the present predicament and evaluate everything objectively. Hence, he finds fault with the Indian way to read history which is replete with obsession attached to past glory: "People with sense of history might have ordered matters differently. But this is precisely the saddening element in Indian history: this absence of growth and development. It is a history whose only lesson is that life goes on. There is only a series of beginning, no final creation" (202). In the same historical context, he has another view of Indian's perpetual sense of tolerance celebrated as a virtue because he finds it originating "from the negative principles" (217). It is because of such misreading of history on India's part that the Indians are rendered "incapable of self-assessment" (216). Nonetheless, his visit to West Bengal provides a few moments of relief. Although he expected Calcutta to be worse than any other Indian city because of his reading of some comments in American magazine describing it as 'the world's most miserable city' and 'the world's last stronghold of Asiatic cholera', he finds touches of grace and elegance there. Yet, Calcutta is only a part of India and hence full of the same squalor and poverty: "With its thin glitter, its filth and overpopulation, its tainted money, its exhaustion, it held the total Indian tragedy and the terrible British failure" (204).

Still the most important visit of Naipaul is made to his ancestral village of Brahmins (Dubeys) in eastern Uttar Pradesh. He is moved by the humility and warmth of his distant relatives; at the same time, he is upset at their ignorance and poverty. An old woman in that village is so much overwhelmed by his visit that he breaks into sobs. But Naipaul's main relative Ramchandra who is away from the village, knocks at his hotel the next day with a bag full of rice, all from his ancestral village. Naipaul wonders what he would do with so much of rice and he reluctantly refuses the gift. Nevertheless, whether the author accepts or not, it is actually a prelude to something else, which Ramchandra hesitates to word out. Finally, it turns out to be a request for sufficient money to file a suit against someone in the village that has an eye on his ancestral land. It is with great difficulty that Naipaul can get rid of this man, though with a sense of reproach and guilt.

Mostly, Naipaul is true to details that any reader who has lived in an Indian village or who has travelled large parts of the country can easily verify. Yet, the facts remains that Naipaul has every little concern for the brighter side of India. He, therefore, has deglamourised the conventional picture of the Taj Mahal. "It is only a despot's monument to a woman...who bore a child every year for fifteen years" (206). Almost the same sense of dismissal is there in his next book, *India: A Wounded Civilization* (1977). Yet, these two books were written with a dark background—in the case of *An Area of Darkness*, it was the defeat of India by China in 1962; in the case of the next book it was the backdrop of Emergency imposed on the country by Mrs. Indira Gandhi. In his final book of the trilogy *India: A Million Mutinies Now* (1990), Naipaul has mellowed down. However, the focus of this paper is the first book where his approach is largely one-sided. The following lines from the book would indicate his inner thought while boarding his train back to England:

> I changed my third class ticket for a first class one, picked my way down dim platforms past the bodies of dogs and men, past third class carriages which were already full and hot. The conductor opened the door of my compartment and I climbed in. I bolted the door, pulled down all the blinds trying to shut out the howls of dogs, shutting out intruders, all those staring faces and skeletal bodies. I put on no lights. I required darkness. (227)

The above statement clearly indicates that Naipaul wants to avoid the third class people of India, wants to escape from the bitter realities, and, hence, he needs darkness to cover himself with even in the prevailing darkness of the country all round.

Prof. R.K. Kaul, in a different context, defends the total attitude of the writer by concluding that Naipaul's outlook is "anti primitivist"[4] and that he is "anti pastoral"[5] in his sentiment. And this way, the writer "sets out systematically to demolish the myth of the noble savage popularised in post Rousseau Europe".[6] In a similar vein, but in the context of *An Area of Darkness*, another critic has pointed out that "His home coming had been an assault on his European styled sensibility".[7] And yet another critic opines that "he has been unable to accept what he has discovered in his ancestor's country".[8]

But all these critics overlook the fact that even Naipaul does not take pleasure in his conclusion about India, whatever is said, is said with pinch of salt; "I did not want India to sink; the mere thought was painful" (243). In like manner he laments the fact that he could not belong to England where he landed as a young lad of eighteen with exhilaration: "I was not English or Indian; I was denied the victories of both" (98). Overall,

Naipaul does not take delight in demeaning India; whenever he finds filth, he does not glamorise it rather he expresses a feeling of regret at this degeneration. He thus admits: "The ugliness was all mine" (256). It is, therefore, inaccurate on the part of critics like C.D. Narasimhaiah to accuse the author of vicariously enjoying a kind of inverted snobbery"[9] and to conclude that "he has a newspaperman's nose for stench".[10] The truth is that the alienated mind of the author does not easily accept the glorified picture of India, which is in conflict with his actual experience of the country. At length, one agrees with the insight of Rajeev Srinivasan after a rereading of Naipaul that Naipaul was not wrong, he merely wrote what he had observed, and he had been horridly disappointed. The culture shock must have been brutal. For India of his imagination and of his ancestral memory of the resplendent culture, was not visible: it was hidden under the weight of a thousand years shame and grime.[11]

From a strong wish to impose himself by being distinctive, by creating a difference and have a sense of full reality of himself, Naipaul ends in a total alienation and utter withdrawal at the end. Beginning with an ardent fervour to belong, and ending with a realization of his incapacity to belong, mostly because of his Western breeding and the subsequent problem of his "unhousedness,"[12] *An Area of Darkness* is at once a highlighter of the darkness within and without. In fact, at several places in the book, the author is aggrieved at the fact that he fails to relate himself to the country of his grandfather because between him and India darkness intervenes. This is an intervening darkness of the "inbetweenness" of the colonial and the postcolonial condition that he carries throughout in his individual and artistic life.

Notes

1. Maya Jaggi, "Nightfall Vision that has Grown ever Darker," *The Guardian*. 12 October, 2001: 1. http://books.guardian.co.uk/news/articles/0610956811800.html
2. C.D. Narasimhaiah, *The Function of Criticism in India: Essays in Indian Response to Literature* (Mysore: Central Institute of Indian Languages, 1986), 124.

3. Naipaul quoted by C.D. Narasimhaiah, 117.
4. R.K. Kaul, "V. S. Naipaul and the Demythologizing of El Dorado" in R.K. Dhawan, 121.
5. *Ibid.*, 122.
6. *Ibid.*, 124.
7. I.K. Masih, 161.
8. Gareth Griffiths, *A Double Exile* (London: Morian Boyars, 1978), 79.
9. C.D. Narasimhaiah, 129.
10. *Ibid.*, 145.
11. Rajeev Srinivasan, "Triumph of the Dispossessed: Naipaul and the Enigma of Exile", 3. http://www.rediff.com/news/2001/Oct/22rajeev.htm
12. Meenakshi Mukherjee, "A House for Mr. Naipaul", *Frontline*, Vol. 18, 22, Oct. 27 Nov. 9, 2001: 1. http://www.flonnet.com/fl1822/18220520.htm

4

Kashmir Across Ages and Beyond Conflicts in the Poetry of Agha Shahid Ali

Jaya Kapoor

Ali's poetry explores some of the deeply layered aspects of the Kashmiri culture where the Hindu and the Muslim aspects were completely intertwined. In the present paper, I explore some of these sacred spaces that he created in his poetry to preserve the unique memories of the land and the culture. He was also simultaneously expressing the pain at the loss of the beauty of the land and the uniqueness of the culture. I will look at various aspects of these poetic spaces, see how they contribute to the Kashmiri heritage and how their loss is also a wearing off of the Kashmiri culture. He used metaphors, images, and mythologies to create a poetic language for him to express this blending. The idea of an ethnic identity of Kashmir had always existed—an identity that had evolved over the centuries shaped by various cultural, political and religious influences. Kashmiri culture has reflected all these elements over the centuries. Mythology and history of the land traces the origin of the land to myths of Hindu Goddess. It is this shared identification that gave Kashmiri culture its distinctive identity. Muslims mostly followers of Sufi sects and the Hindu Pandits shared a history and identified with myths and traditions of this shared past. Ali also talks about this identity in his poetry. When he left the valley in the 80s and moved to Delhi, there was a rising discontent with the political situation in the valley but the situation was still not completely out of control and there was also no inkling of the turmoil the coming decade would see. Till the mid-eighties, the manifestations of the problem were also political and left the lives of the common people of Kashmir relatively untouched. By the mid-eighties the common people began to feel the heat when the political matter was sought to be resolved through militant ways. And then in the early years of 1990s came the eruption of violence in Kashmir. The insurgency instigated and fuelled by Pakistan crippled life in the state. There was political turmoil and disturbance. Processions and demonstrations for Azad Kashmir were held across the state. Taking advantage of the situation, vested interests targeted the Kashmiri Pandits who were compelled to flee the valley and migrate to the plains. Of a population of 200,000 pandits, only about 10,000 remained in the valley (Madan 25). Their houses were torched down and their property looted. The State Government was suspended and President's rule imposed in the state. The army moved in to restore order and control the situation. It had great difficulty in distinguishing between militants and terrorists who often used common people as human shields. There was an atmosphere of mistrust which was stoked up further by inflammatory messages and rumours against the army presence in the valley. There were also human rights violations on the part of the army in its attempt to restore order and flush out militants from among the common innocent citizens. There was a huge backlash of public opinion against the violations. Life in the valley came to a standstill. This was the phase when there was a complete shutdown of all postal and communication services in the valley.

The shutdown in the valley could be seen as a moment of rupture in this narrative. Shahid loved Kashmir and reflected the pain of the land in his poetry. As his homeland went up in flames of violence, his poetry reflected the ashes left behind. The letters and phone calls were not only a way of getting news from friends and family for Ali. They were also like a lifeline—the umbilical cord—that kept his connection with his motherland alive. The shutdown was a period of great anxiety for him especially because of the state of conflict in the valley. When he went back to the valley for his annual visit, what he saw shocked him. The atmosphere was tense, the army presence was quite conspicuous, the curfew, the burnt houses and the exodus of the Pandits had changed the entire topography of his beloved city.

Under these conditions, it would be easy to take sides and become political. And it is most difficult not to be political and still be involved. When he quotes Mandelstam in the opening poem of the *The Country without a Postoffice*—"We shall meet again, in Petersburg,...", the subtext could be interpreted as his attempt to retain a voice of sanity in the mayhem. Mandelstam had not succumbed to the power politics of Stalin's Russia and had refused to tow the party line. He wrote poetry that was reflective of a deep humanism in its philosophy. His art did not forward any agenda. And this deeply humanistic vision is to be seen in Ali's poetry as well. There is no political posturing of any kind. He only reflects the trauma of his land and his people in his poetry. He had once said in a conversation with Ghosh that he could be the national poet of Kashmir but would not like to be the nationalist poet. And there lies the vast difference of poetic vision in the fine distinction of words. He is not at any point of time an advocate of the secessionist forces. He also does not have a public stand vis-à-vis the political movement in Kashmir. If anything, he was very deeply disturbed by the events in the valley, but he also recognized the uniqueness and beauty of the Kashimiri heritage. It was this that he saw being wrecked and that he evokes again and again in his poetry, trying to bring together all that he felt was a symbol of that heritage, of that homeland. Kashmir becomes a heritage that Ali is attempting to preserve in his poetry.

Ali felt that the events in Kashmir were damaging the Kashmiri culture that had evolved over the centuries. Kashmiri culture had been very deeply influenced by the Sufi sect. There was an increasing interference of the Wahabis who declared the Sufi sect as un-Islamic, since it created mediators between man and God where none existed.

The use of Mandelstam's line—"We shall meet again, in Petersburg,..." sets the frame within which Srinagar could be seen. "When you leave home in the morning, you never know if you'll return" is his perception of the situation there. His voice tries to call out all the names people have known the land by from mythological to present across the lands. Now he feels that the oppressive atmosphere of the place has taken away the right to choose an identity—"Kashmir, Kaschmir...Kerseymere?" (Ali 171). The people are issued identity cards and passes but this is not a security against being taken in for an interrogation "Srinagar was under curfew. The identity passes may or may not have helped in the crackdown" (Ali 172). The insecurity of leaving home never to come back is brought out again in a later poem in the figure of Rizwan. The description opens in a probable interrogation camp in a cantonment area where a young boy succumbs to torture and his family will never know of his death. "Drippings from a suspended burning tire/ are falling on the back of a prisoner,/ the naked boy/ screaming, 'I know nothing'" (Ali 178). The figure is recognized as Rizwan and suddenly the trauma becomes personal for the poet "Rizwan, it's you, Rizwan, it's you" I cry out/ as he steps closer, the sleeves of his phiren torn./ "Each night put Kashmir in your dreams," he says,/ then touches me, his hands crusted with snow,/ whispers, "I have been cold a long long time" (Ali 179). The last words could have multiple meanings—is he cold from the torture, was he dead and thrown in the mountains a long time back, or because he was drowned half dead in the waters of Jhelum. In *The Last Saffron,* he mentions the tabloids of missing boys who could be found floating in the Jhelum "the Jhelum flows under them, sometimes with a dismembered body", connecting them to the figure of Rizwan. The sense of oppression is highlighted by the fact that even placing wreaths on tombs is banned there. The description is followed by another description of a demonstration dispersed by soldiers leaving behind the shoes and blood and the sound of mourning mothers resounding the streets. The mourning mothers occur in the Prologue where the lines "Blessed women rub the ashes together" where "son after son—never to return from the night of torture—was taken away" (Ali 172) bringing the figure of Rizwan to mind again. The desolation of the land resounds in *Muharram in Srinagar, 1992* with "streets bereft of children: they are dead, not asleep" where men have all vanished leaving the women behind wondering "O, when will our hands return, if only broken?" (Ali 234). He mentions

Rizwan's death again in *Dear Shahid* "You must have heard Rizwan was killed. Rizwan: Guardian of the gates of Paradise" (Ali 194). The houses and the neighbourhood have been routinely found to catch fire at night. They could have been torched down by the army or by the insurgents—Shahid makes no comment. He only says "...snow begins to fall/ on us like ash. Black on the edges of flames, it cannot extinguish the neighbourhoods,/ the homes set ablaze by midnight soldiers./ Kashmir is burning" (Ali 179). Ali understands that the damage to the cultural inheritance is irredeemable and the process is irreversible. He finds a comparison of the fires with the floods in the myth of Noah in *The City of Daughters*. He uses the lines by Baldwin to open the poem and then the phrase "no more water" runs like a refrain through the poem "No More Water!—We again plant embers./ what's left to abolish in Lal Chowk?... A tree bursts into branches of smoke.... From the tree we are tearing flowers of smoke" (Ali 233). Fire is burning the valley down and it seems like the wrath of God is falling on Earth—on the Paradise on Earth. And as the valley burns, the palm ashes from the mourning rituals of Ash Wednesday turn into the ashes of the Chinar—the tree that along with the poplars covers the valley and constitutes the essence of the nature in the valley. With the news of deaths and interrogations, demonstrations and police action, comes the news of the houses in downtown Srinagar being torched down "The rubble of downtown Srinagar stares at me from *The Times*" (Ali 173). There is an all-pervasive presence of the army and convoys move about on its roads and soldiers sit in bunkers dotting the city scape. He gets desperate calls from back home making him painfully conscious of the distance across the lands "See how your world has cracked./ Why aren't you here? Where are you? Come back./ is history deaf there across the oceans?" he is asked and another letter he receives says "here one can't even manage postage stamps...today I went to the post office.... Bags and bags...all undelivered mail...I saw this letter addressed to you. I am enclosing it. I hope it's from someone you are longing for news of" (Ali 194). These letters become not only means of communication but cries of pain "I read them, letters of lovers.... Calls to prayer/ to deaf worlds across continents...and my lament is cries countless, cries like dead letters sent to this world whose end was near, always near" (Ali 205). The voice is that of the tourist guide who acts as the muezzin and his call to prayer becomes a cry of pain. He tells of the previous muezzin's death to the poet. In the long list of the dead, Ali makes a special mention of the death of the muezzin "when the muezzin/ died, the city was robbed of every Call" (Ali 202). The call of the muezzin is a unique tradition in Kashmir where along with the *azaan*, verses are recited in praise of God in the Sufi tradition introduced by Hazrat Ali Hamdani, a great sufi thinker and writer—"he introduced in the mosques the loud, collective chanting of litanies in praise of God and the Prophet before every prayer, the *aurad-i-fathiyya*, resembling the chanting of mantras in Hindu temples in Kashmir. The practice is still followed in Kashmir till today, and is a distinguishing feature of Islam in the area, being unknown elsewhere" (Sikand Rao 494). The tradition has been put under a scanner by advocates of purist Islamic practices. The tradition gets lost with the death of the muezzin in these lines. Ali remembers Shah Hamdan in a touching reference "I've tied a knot with green thread at Shah Hamdan, to be untied when the atrocities are stunned by your jewelled return" (Ali 180). He also weaves in the memories of many other sufi saints of the valley in his poetry. Lal Ded or Lalla was a great saint who was deeply influenced by Hamdani, though she herself belonged to the Hindu Shaiva sect. She had simplified some complex Shaivite practices and made them accessible to the common people.

She is also closely associated with the sufi saints, the most prominent being Hazrat Nuruddin Nurani commonly known as Nund Rishi. He had been instrumental in spreading Islam in the valley the rishis preached in the language of the people and the poetic compositions of Nund Rishi were given the status of *Koshur Quran* or the Kashmiri commentary on the Muslim holy scripture. He is mentioned as a true disciple of Lalla or Lal Ded by Ali "Was it thus/ that Lal Ded—robed in brilliant green/ of paradise—rose from her ashes.... She blessed her true heir: Sheikh Noor-ud-din/ he still speaks through five centuries of poets" the shrine of Sheikh Noor-ud-din was burnt down in a confrontation between the army and the insurgents. And he mourns the loss in the voice of the saint himself "Fire moves on its quick knees-/ through Charar-i-Sharif toward my shrine.... Alas! Death has bent my back./ it is too late for threads at Charar-i-Sharif". Amidst these images of the mourning saints of the Kashmiri tradition he places the figure of Hubba Khatun "the peasant girl who became the queen" (Ali 172) and whose voice represents the protest of the people even now. Her songs are still sung by the women in Kashmir. Ali says her songs "have re-echoed for four hundred years, the songs of Hubba Khatun... her grief, alive to this day, in her own roused the people into frenzied opposition to the Mughal rule.... Each fall they sing her songs" (Ali 173). The Shalimar Gardens are the epitome of the Mughal presence in Kashmir and Ali talks about them in *Son et lumiere at Shalimar Garden*. The poem is a link between various threads of Kashmir's history. He mentions the mythical story of the creation of the valley from a lake by Goddess Sharika who slayed the demon Jalodbhavaby who was believed to be invincible under water. She drained the great lake and took the form of a bird and dropped a pebble on him that became a hill and crushed him. The mythical past from the Hindu tradition is brought in again in *History of Paisley*. The paisley is a symbol of the footprints of Goddess Parvati made when she was running away from lord Shiva after a quarrel. And the river Jhelum was a commemoration of their subsequent union and runs through the valley in the shape of a paisley. The motif of the paisley is widely recognized as a typical motif of Kashmiri craft. Most of these craftsmen are Muslims but the origin of the motif as Ali puts it is "these/ are her footprints from the day the world bean/ when the land rushed, from the ocean...refugee from her lord.... And there in the valley below, the river/ beguiled its banks into petrified longing" (Ali 218). The motifs were woven into delicate shawls that were sold across the world by the Kashmiri traders— "your gauze of cloud thrown/ off your shoulders over the vale" (Ali 219). Now these motifs are no more found on the carpets woven by the weavers but reflected in the bloody footprints of protesters who could be these weavers "Look! Their feet bleed; they leave footprints on the street/ which will give up its fabric, at dusk, a carpet..." (Ali 218). With the disturbances and the attempts to deny the Hindu myths as a part of Kashmiri history, Ali feels this beautiful aspect of the heritage will be lost "Do you hear her bells?/ O, alibi of chronology, in what script/ in your ledger will this narrative be lost?" But with the disruption of life, even that craft suffers and the craftsmen can no longer work as before "The gauze is torn.... The city burns" (Ali 219). Amidst these grief torn voices Ali also talks of his traumatic visit to his own house in Srinagar in *Return to Harmony 3*. The house was one of the three houses built among beautiful gardens where Shahid's father and his brothers lived. When the family left the Valley and the army moved in, the house was occupied and a part of it converted into an office. He is greeted like a trespasser in his own house "A bunker has put the house under a spell. Shadowed eyes watch me open the gate, like a trespasser" (Ali 199). There were once acres of beautiful gardens surrounding the houses but now the house is only a bunker. The gardens are perceived to be a security threat and have been burnt down "troops will burn down the garden and let the haven remain... the fate of Paradise" (Ali 199). The run down gardens also lead to the question about the whereabouts of the gardener "Has the gardener fled...was the gardener killed?/ And the postman?" The place is more or less intact. The Quran is still in the drawer where his mother had kept it, the phone is dead reminding him of the broken communication links of the valley, the mountains are covered with snow, not coloured with blood as it so often is now, the picture of the parents as a young couple reminds of an early poem by Ali "A Lost Memory of Delhi". And by the closing lines the long long wait of the house for its people erupts "the house begins to shake in my arms, and when the armed world is still again, with pity, it is the house that is holding me in its arms and the cry coming faded from its empty rooms is my cry" (Ali 199). The house becomes a refuge, a bond and a presence of all that is gone—the people and the times. In *Some Vision of the World Cashmere*, he remembers the outhouse where his grandmother used to live and which has been occupied by the army "dust everywhere, on old phones, on damp files, on broken desks. In her drawing room a clerk types" (Ali 188). When her dead body is brought into the house, "the mirrors have grieved in her absence. They run to greet her at the door. It is her home again" (Ali 189). He feels "I am holding her hand in that sun which is shining on all summers of my childhood...and she is telling me *God is merciful, God is compassionate*" (Ali 189).

Kashmiri Pandits are a very important aspect of the Kashmiri identity and Ali talks about their migration from the valley again and again. In *I See Kashmir from New Delhi at Midnight,* he talks about their migration "By that dazzling light/ we see men removing statues from temples./ We beg them, 'Who will protect us if you leave?'/ They don't answer, they just disappear/ on the road to the plains, clutching the gods." The Hindu gods as protectors of the valley and the Rizwan whose name means protector, blend in an image of loss here. One is a target of the terrorists and the other is the innocent victim of state action against the terrorists. The words from Tacitus the central idea evolves "They make a desolation and call it peace" (Ali 175) one side is trying to carve an independent nation based on ethnic identity but massacres and drives out the Hindus who are integral to this ethnic identity. The other side puts the valley under curfew and tries to project a picture of peace. Just as the Roman claim to empire was decried through the words of Tacitus, Ali refutes the authenticity of both sides in Kashmir and questions their claims to authority with these words. He realized that this was a huge cultural and historical loss for the valley—"at a certain point I lost track of you/ You needed me. You needed to perfect me:/ In your absence you polished me into the Enemy" (Ali 176). The history of the valley is not that of only Muslims or only of the Hindus. It is made from strands of both the faiths. A loss of any one is the loss of both because they are inseparable—"Your history gets in the way of my memory/ I am everything you lost. Your perfect enemy./ Your memory gets in the way of my memory" (Ali 177).

He knows that the wounds that the displacement has left on the mind and heart of the Kashmiri Pandits will never go away. What they have lost is not just life and property, the loss of trust is a much bigger loss. Even if the displaced families come back, life will never be the same again. If they had not been forced to migrate from their homeland, probably the problem in Kashmir could have found a solution, at least things would have been different from what they are now when liberal voices do not have any place there: "I'm everything you lost./ I hid my pain even from myself; I revealed my pain only to myself./ There is everything to forgive. You can't forgive me./ If only somehow you could have been mine,/ what would not have been possible in the world?" (Ali 177).

He realized that the loss of trust that the migration had created cannot be undone. Kashmir like the rest of North India after Partition will forever have to bear the pain of loss of brothers and those who have lost their all can never bring themselves to come back without knotted relations. Once life looses its simplicity and relations assume complications, they can never be brought back to their phase of innocence and simplicity. It is never very easy to forgive and forgetting is impossible. "You won't forgive me./ My memory keeps getting in the way of your history./ There is nothing to forgive. You can't forgive me" (Ali 177). The same emotion that permeates all partition literature is reflected in the words of Shahid: "In the lake the arms of temples and mosques are locked/ in each other's reflections./ Have you soaked saffron for them when they are/ Found like this centuries later in this country/ I have stitched to your shadow?" (Ali 177).

The closing lines of "After August Wedding in Lahore, Pakistan" his turmoil comes through clearly. The old century moves into a new one and brings new hopes and new joys, but the pain in the valley only gets more acute—"It is pain/ from which love departs into all new pain:/ Freedom's terrible thirst, flooding Kashmir,/ is bringing love to its tormented glass... of what shall I not sing, and sing." With these lines, having crossed the rivers of fire and destruction, he is finally able to utter the sacred words he had found himself unable to speak in the opening poem of the collection "and that Blessed word with no meaning—who will utter it?" (Ali 173). What he talks of here is probably the freedom of Kashmir to an ethnic identity. He does not support the bloodshed from either the insurgents or the state. He only wants to preserve a cultural tradition that forces talking of religious identity or nationalist identity seem to be subsuming. He probably realises the futility of it when he says "of what shall I not sing", though he knows he must sing the songs of the life of the valley that is fast getting lost and that is more precious, beautiful and fragile than freedom probably.

Nawaz Gul Qanungo quotes Utathya, a young researcher among the audience at a meeting in JNU on the tenth death anniversary of Shahid, as saying: Shahid, at some level, was able to remove the hegemony that India and Pakistan had traditionally imposed on the Kashmir discourse. Leaving the state aside, Shahid's poetry made his Indian and Pakistani audience feel Kashmiri as a Kashmiri would feel while reading him.

Works Cited

Ali, Agha Shahid. *The Veiled Suite.*

Ghosh, Amitav. *The Ghat of the Only World*, www.amitavghosh.com

Qanungo, Nawaz Gul. www.kashmirlit.org/remembering-agha-shahid-ali

5

V.S. Naipaul as a Diasporic Writer with Special Reference to *A House for Mr. Biswas*

Sunita Rai

V.S. Naipaul is acknowledged as a writer of diaspora who is in search of roots. A Trinidadian by birth, Indian by descent and Western by education and attitude, Naipaul strives to carve out a space for himself. Naipaul's creative urge can be interpreted in the modern context of colonial consciousness. He makes us aware of the Indian immigrant's dilemma, his troubles and travails in the rapidly changing Caribbean universe. *A House for Mr. Biswas* is a treatise on the pangs of exile. It is a critique of the problems and plight of the Indian or Hindu community in Trinidad in general and a life sketch of Naipaul's father in particular.

Vidiadhar Surajprasad's *A House for Mr. Biswas* deals with the predicament of the unanchored souls. The idea of India exists in the minds of the diaspora through forms of spatial displacement in which the originary sacred sites of India are transformed into the local. This form of transference of space means that India gets internalized and then projected on to another geographical space without so much as a hint of dissonance. The source text of the originary symbol is, however, not the text of Sanskrit high culture but 'degraded' epic fragments from the *Ramcharitmanasa* of Tulsidas as memorially reconstructed by the indentured labourers. Consequently, the grand Indian Epic itself gets written out in the 'infinitely reproducible space' of Hanuman house in *A House for Mr. Biswas*.

A House for Mr. Biswas (1961), the most celebrated novel of V.S. Naipaul—traces the struggle of Mr. Mohun Biswas to own a house which he ultimately does manage to acquire, in the process losing the security of an extended Indian family. Based upon the life of his father, the novel records the struggles of the East Indian immigrants in Trinidad to become part of the national community. The life-story of Mr. Biswas shows a self-respecting individual's rebellion against tyranny. The possession of a private dwelling becomes his goal in life. It leads to isolation, dispossession and various disillusionments.

Naipaul was born in Trinidad, a West Indian Island on August 17, 1932. His grandfather, a Banaras-trained Brahmin, had emigrated to Trinidad as an indentured labourer. He wrote about him:

> The Americans do not want me because I am too British. The public here do not want me because I am too foreign. (15 August 1958: 5)

To be an expatriate is to be conscious of being one, and this consciousness manifests itself in a variety of ways: a sense of loss and dispossession, a feeling of remaining straddled between two cultures and anxiety to belong—either to one's native cultural milieu or to the new environment, an assertion of one's nativity or immigrant status; an attempt to turn one's liminality into strength, an agenda of multiculturalism, an active interrogation of all notions of belonging, an insistent celebration of 'unbelonging', and an ultimate urgency to prove oneself.

At the heart of this expatriate consciousness is the issue of identity. The story of Mr. Biswas is the story of a lowborn Indian's absurd yet heroic struggle for identity and independence in colonial Trinidad. There is the predicament of the Indian, indentured under a cheating contract and marooned in an inhospitable land. According to David Ormerod:

> Naipaul's world is one of homeless nomadic migrants, making a middle passage from Africa or India to the West Indies, thence to England and back again, for, after three hundred years, there is no society and no system of values in which they can take root.

> Against this indistinct and dissolving background, the characters try to seize upon something to give permanence and to arrest flux—
>
> Mr. Biswas' desire for a house,... (1968: 162)

Biswas's character shows enormous resilience and a capacity for growth. The terrible inheritance of the past is not denied, but a few possibilities are also revealed through Mr. Biswas's quest for a dignified existence. '*Biswas*' in Hindi means 'faith'. In Tulsidom, he alone fights in his own ludicrous and brave way the vulgar, emasculating Tulsi Machinery. His struggles are heroic in a world where there no heroes. So it becomes an ordinary, obscure man's struggle against overwhelming odds. Because the battle involves the conflict between identity and non-entity, and because Biswas does this with an inner belief, his simple acts are deeply moving.

What gives significance to the quality of Biswas's experience is his persistent desire to understand life and to make sense of a chaotic world. This is an infinitely difficult task for a character who is historically displaced and lives in a destitute society in a derelict land. He is an orphan in more than one sense. The central, integrating and ever-expanding metaphor is the house. As Biswas moves from one strange house to another—be it his father's hut or the 'alien fortress' called Hanuman House—the metaphor gathers meanings and resonances that give a quality of mythical significance to an individual's experience. The final possession of the house, flawed though it must be, is a truly 'stupendous' achievement. Amidst the family, and amongst a lifetime's acquisitions, it stands out:

> But bigger than them all was the house, his house. How terrible it would have been at this time, to be without it:
>
> ...worse, to have lived without even attempting to lay claim to one's portion of the earth, to have lived and died as one had been born, unnecessary and unaccommodated.

Even for the children the house provided an ordered world, something missed in Biswas's past:

> Soon it seemed to the children that they had never lived anywhere but in the tall square house in Sikkim Street.

> From now on their lives will be ordered, their memories coherent. (2011: 614)

It is in this environment the children will discover themselves spiritually and aesthetically. It is at this human level the house becomes the central symbol of the novel with universal applicability. We realise, like Mr. Biswas, that we are all dying in mortgaged houses, we are all, all our lives 'stiffening in rented mansions', though some of us, like Mr. Biswas, may be lucky enough to have our own laburnum tree. Naipaul's shaping imagination has through this metaphor seen beyond the particular and given it the dimension of a universal symbol. The house becomes the creative and positive side of his rebellion. It acquires dimensions of his own identity. The final triumph of his own house is Mr. Biswas's most meaningful, though ambiguous achievement and in that metaphor lies the book's most enduring, human significance.

In *A House for Mr. Biswas*, Naipaul shows how the expatriate Hindu society in Trinidad loses its traditional customs and beliefs under the impact of the West-Oriented Creole culture of the island. Mr. Biswas is a Trinidad Hindu, but he is born when the thinking of his society has already moved towards the West and away from India. The rituals are still practised but the meaning has gone out of them. Even in the Hanuman House of the orthodox Tulsi family, Hindu *puja* is mixed with the observance of Christian customs and festivals. Mrs. Tulsi sends her sons to the Roman Catholic College in Port of Spain and allows them to perform Hindu *puja* even when they are wearing crucifixes. Her daughter Chinta, uses Hindu incantations in combination with a candle and a crucifix. When sickness strikes the Tulsi family, Hindu prayers, Indian and African superstition and Western science are all called upon to contribute their complementary offices. The Tulsis celebrate Christ's birthday, in good Creole Style, with English apples, cakes and ice cream, and Portuguese Cherry brandy. Less Hindi is spoken now and Trinidad Creole English holds sway. But, while the young are caught in strong cultural cross-currents and cease to dream of a return to India, the old Hindus continue to see themselves, although far from the motherland, cast in the role of the last bastions of the old, pure and the noble culture.

> In the arcade of Hanuman House...there was already the evening assembly of old men.... They could not speak English and were not interested in the land where they lived; it was a place where they had come for a short time and stayed longer than they expected.
>
> They continually talked of going back to India, but when the opportunity came, many refused, afraid of the unknown, afraid to leave the familiar temporariness. And every evening they came to the arcade of the solid, friendly house, smoked, told stories, and continued to talk of India. (2011: 201)

The Tulsis likewise looked on their stay in Arwacas as "no more than a stage in the journey that had begun when Pundit Tulsi left India". Like the generation he represents, Mr. Biswas began to realise that he would not return to India; he had to make his home in Trinidad. However, from the first he was stricken with the same malady as the Tulsis and the old men. The hut where he lived with his old mother was 'a temporary arrangement'. When he contemplated each action, it was no longer merely action, it became symbolic of a greater futility, of his lost happiness, and his isolation from any significant life. He must escape the immediate because he cannot accept the absurdity of the existential position. Mr. Biswas then has no roots in the land or customs of his forefathers, and the New World of Trinidad seems to throw him off. Yet he did not want to have lived without even attempting to lay claim to his portion of the earth; to have lived and died as he had been born unnecessary and unaccommodated. In his attempts to build a house, we can see his desire to assert his own significance and to establish a small centre or order in a society that had no rules and patterns.

The organising theme of the work is the idea of slavery—slavery as the essence of the historical experience. Naipaul explores the consciousness of those who have escaped historical slavery but carry about them the mark, in their attitudes and sensibilities and convictions, of the slaves, the unnecessary man. The theme is developed in a multitude of details, ideas, and images enacted in the organisation of the Tulsi family. It is a microcosm of a slave society. Hanuman House—the name is carefully chosen for its ironic and metaphorical purposes—has a mythical dimension as well for Hanuman is the Supreme Servant of Rama in the *Ramayana.* Biswas's attempt to escape the confines of this stifling 'alien fortress' is the effort of slaves and coolies to escape from their inhuman bondage, whether from the chains of injustice, of slavery or caste.

While slavery is the implicit force in the novel, it is the character of Biswas and his Hindu world that give the work its other resonances. Naipaul makes the struggle of Biswas so compelling and convincing because he establishes the suffocating, Hindu world with vividness and fidelity. Against the solidity of this world, Mr. Biswas's efforts acquire heroic dimensions. It is only when the claustrophobic world is coming apart that Biswas feels some sense of freedom: his artistic gift-sign painting-leads to his doom and later comes to his rescue. From disintegrating communalism the novel moves to displaced individualism. It is a gradual growth for it encompasses a whole culture, a people's whole history. As a result the labourer became—

> A derelict man in a derelict land; a man discovering himself, with surprise and resignation, lost in a landscape which had never ceased to be unreal because the scene of an enforced and always temporary residence; the slaves kidnapped from one continent and abandoned on the unprofitable plantations of another, from which there could never more be escape. (1962: 190)

A House for Mr. Biswas is the story of a lowborn man's effort to overcome the derelict land of Trinidad's East Indian community, and it is fitting that it should open with description of an old man dying stranded in an arid landscape; Bipti's father, futile with asthma, propped himself up on his string bed and said, "Fate. There is nothing we can do about it." Fate had brought him from India to the sugar estate, aged him quickly and left to die in a crumbling mud hut in the swamplands; yet he spoke of Fate often and affectionately, as though merely by surviving, he had been particularly favoured. In such a landscape Bipti's father had only one objective—to survive—and he has done this with the passive acceptance. The Indian capacity to accept suffering with passive resignation helped them to hang on, but in doing so, ensured that they would build a society which the creative writer could regard only with despair. Such is Naipaul's view, and he remarks on:

> The saddening element in Indian History: this absence of growth and development. It is a history whose only lesson is that life goes on. There is only a series of beginnings, no final creation. (1964: 212-13)

The terrible inheritance of the past is not denied, but a few possibilities are also revealed through Mr. Biswas's quest for a dignified existence. Biswas's character shows enormous resilience and a capacity for growth. This springs from an inner faith in the value of human personality. The house in *A House for Mr. Biswas* stands for what life has denied to its lowborn hero in a poverty-stricken colonial set-up.

There are two great obstacles Mr. Biswas has to overcome in order to achieve his goal. The first is to conquer the fatalistic, passive attitude bequeathed from his ancestors; the second is to break away from an oppressively traditional society, itself in the process of decay. The hostility of fate is an idea handed down in Mr. Biswas's family from one generation to another. His struggle to achieve identity and independence in a colonial set-up seems to have failed, but despite the death in debt and the last days, clouded with worry over the future of his son, Anand, Mr. Biswas has in fact triumphed. In however insignificant a way, his attainment of the house ideal is an assertion of his will to be different, to control his environment rather than to be manipulated or controlled by it.

The corrosive impact of Western education on the Hindu way of life cannot be underestimated. It is, for instance, Mr. Biswas's exposure to Western education at the Canadian Mission School at Pagotes which makes him think differently from his illiterate brothers and inspires him to live a life different from theirs. Indeed, Western education becomes the only saviour of the expatriate Indians in Port of Spain where there is no

Hanuman House to protect them. That is why he leaves no stone unturned for the sake of his children's education. But Western education alienates the Trinidad Indians from their cultural roots.

Since the Hindu way of life symbolised by Hanuman House in Arwacas is largely a rural way, it does not withstand the impact of urbanization. His obvious rusticity, his race in its relation to the white community, his poverty and his social awkwardness make him ill at ease in the multiracial society of the capital city. He now finds himself in a world dominated by European values and ideas—spacious and luxuriously furnished buildings, orderly lawns and gardens, the new and glistening and a world of antiseptic cleanliness. It is a world of exquisite class-consciousness, which is why he suffers when Shama makes a grammatical mistake in speaking to Miss Logie. It consists of various races uprooted from their original societies and abandoned on an alien landscape, with little in common and without the resources to create a new energetic society. There are the European settlers who eat and drink grossly, pay no heed to the economic and cultural progress of the region and claim status on the basis of their white race. There are the African Negroes who imitate the lifestyle of their enslavement to them. There are the Indian labourers who are a peasant-minded, money-minded community, spiritually static because cut off from its roots, its religion reduced to rites without philosophy. Naipaul's encounter with India and many other lands is a kind of homecoming. The truth is that a writer like Naipaul can only find a house not a home. The memory of home becomes a paramount in narratives where home itself is but a memory. This sense of alienation is also the writer's sense of a new being, the artist's vision of a new reality. And therein lies the Naipaulian knot, travelling everywhere, belonging nowhere.

Mr. Biswas's life and achievement portrayed in the novel become a kind of Odyssey of perennial restless quest. The novel is a moving critique of Biswas's experience of alienation and exile. The protagonist's owning a house underlines the protagonist's dignity, integrity, and struggle for identity. House stands for the image of fulfilment and a release from slavery and tyranny of an extended family. As a matter of fact, house in the novel is a symbol for freedom, from slavery and oppression.

Works Cited

Naipaul, V.S. *A House for Mr. Biswas*. Picador, 2011.

———. *London, The Times Literary Supplement.* 15 August 1958; rep. *Critical Perspective V.S. Naipaul*, ed. Richard D. Hammer. London: Heinemann, 1977.

———. *The Middle Passage*. London: Penguin, 1962.

———. *An Area of Darkness*. London, 1964.

Ormerod, David. *In a Derelict Land: The Novels of V.S. Naipaul.* 1968.

6

V.S. Naipaul's Concept of Diaspora

Sanjay Swarnkar

The word 'diaspora' is derived from the Greek word 'diaspeirein' which means disperse or scatter. The word 'diaspora' originally referred to the dispersal of Jews as a result of the Roman Victory of Jerusalem. The Jews were driven from their own country and their dispersal was a mass migration. "The second and the widely known meaning of diaspora refer to the setting of scattered colonies of Jews outside Palestine after the Babylonian exile."[1] The first recorded usage of the word 'diaspora' in English language was in 1876 referring to the refuges of the Irish famine. The term was widely assimilated by the mid-1950s, with long-term expatriates in significant numbers from other particular countries like England, USA and so on. In all cases, the term 'diaspora' carries a sense of displacement and finds itself separated from its national territory.

The Third World diasporic writings have got their roots in the postcolonial condition. The present meaning and connotation of the word diaspora is the dispersal of intellectuals particularly authors who came abroad in order to search new themes regarding their works. Thus, they became a part of diaspora in foreign land with different sociological, historical, ethnic and contemporary factors that go into the make up of diasporas.

It is clear that 'diaspora' and diasporic writing has got wide ranging connotations of intricacies, some of which defy simple explanation. For example, India, Africa, West Indies and Canada have special diasporic backgrounds through which the writers' works throw light on different issues. In the postcolonial world, the diasporic writing has come to the front. Many Third World's colonies writers have migrated to the developed countries where English was being spoken and they have become the part of that culture, they have adopted and nevertheless they could not separate themselves from the culture to which they belong.

Twentieth-century writing particularly after when the World War II was over, is primarily associated with the diaspora. The uprooting of the British Empire after World War II had already given a chance of conglomeration of different races, religions, creeds and even sexes. This fusion of different factors gave birth to the diasporic culture and literature in the world since 1950.

Vidiadhar Surajprasad Naipaul is one of the best living diasporic authors of the world. He is the mixture of four cultures—his Indian forefathers, his experiences in Trinidad, his literary training and first marriage in England with Patricia Hale and lastly his attraction towards the Islamic world of his marriage in the later stage with a Pakistani journalist Nadira Albi. In this way, we find that he is a product of hybrid culture and a beautiful flower of the diaspora transcending the bindings and limitations of countries, castes, races and even religions.

In the first place, it is important to understand that Naipaul does not represent a racial diaspora in the sense in which Africans (Afro Caribbeans) do. Naipaul belongs to the East Indian Caribbean 'sub-diaspora abroad' and he seems to be the sole author of his stature and experience to have worked (or is still working) on the grounds of that complex intermingling in the overall Caribbean historical journey. His migration is identifiable with the same migration of other Caribbean authors. The difference takes place in his distancing and excluding himself from that literary phenomenon in highly and individual terms and this has also assisted him in constructing his own kind of psychological explanation about his individual, familiar and literary burdens to feel the ambition to be an author and it is clear in his works—*Finding the Centre, The Enigma of Arrival, A Stay in the World*:

> The History I carried with me together with the self-awareness that had come with my education and ambition, had sent me into the world with a sense of glory dead....[2]

Naipaul is the product of the postcolonial scenario and he has always tried his best to imbibe more cultures, races and religions in his personality along with his writings. His is a beautiful instance of how one author carrying within him a burden of race, language, history and an individual ambition, searches for a viable convention with a knowledge that he is an ex-colonial individual at a point in history. He appears intellectually to retrace what happened to a whole gamut of nationalities, culture, races and people. His compulsive journeys through the leftover territories of the Empire and his dark peregrinations in search for literary correlatives—India, Caribbean, Africa, Latin America, the Islamic world multiplied and accentuated his creative burdens and stern conclusions about things. The following quotations from *Finding the Centre* throws light on his search for 'Centre' of order, the process of the growth of knowledge:

> A writer after a time carries his world with him, his own burden of experience (one deepening the others); and I do believe...that I would have found equivalent connections with my past wherever I went.[3]

Naipaul's writing contains the finest examples of travel, fiction, autobiography and his imaginary personages. His Indian impressions are the most beautiful products of his major novels in which he has expressed his diasporic concerns and selected the matter which creates the best fictional creations in his novels. The diasporic materials in his novels as well as in the autobiographical writing throw light on a wide panorama of the characters and their behaviours which is the part of the diasporic world. The creation of a diasporic material was for Naipaul a process through accompanied his idea of not having a literary model, a tradition or a viable subject matter.

In *The Mimic Men* Naipaul's basic quarrel with history that he knew and belonged to, is the lack of anything positive and worth celebrating, what is left is only a residue of European exploitation and brutality in islands like the ones in the Caribbean. His lack of having any constructive or positive part is connected with this non-availability to the writer for patterning a logical or a moral paradigm of visions and values. He says:

> In England I was also a colonial, out of the stresses of that and out of my worship of the name of the writer, I had without knowing it fallen into the error of thinking of writing as a kind of display.[4]
>
> ...I couldn't be a writer in the same way, because to be a colonial, as I was, was to be spared knowledge. It was to live in an intellectually restricted way: it was to accept those restrictions....[5]

Naipaul remained a rootless wanderer in search of his own identity. For it he visited many countries even continents, small islands, small and big towns and even tiny villages in India to search out his own roots and to express himself as a man of personality. But he could not associate himself with any culture, nationality or even religion. His own writings—articles, interviews, journalistic pieces—illustrate his attitude about the impossibility of finding a literary ancestry, a suitable lineage to authenticate his kind of mixed and amorphous, experience. In his early articles—"London", "Jasmine" and "The Regional Barrier", he talked about the difficulty of an outsider's appreciation of his "social comedies" without the knowledge of the region he wrote about. The comment, "The English language was mine, and tradition was not",[6] conveys his persistent hammering of the same kind of split as a migrant diasporic writer living in an uneasy relationship with two apparent problems. He called himself an "Exotic" writer whose works could not get recognition due to the break from mainstream convention of Europe. It is worth nothing that though Trinidad was a colony in 1950s, his fictional works were not seen as a regional expression of geographic space of the Empire. It was perceived as foreign, though stylistically Naipaul was writing out of European and specially British Literary tradition.

As a product of diaspora, he is a real cosmopolitan man who individually does not believe in caste, creed, sex and even in nationality. The only problem with V.S. Naipaul was that he could not associate himself with any culture, nationality or even religion. He is a skeptic and non-believer. His early works, the satirical comedies are based a good deal on calypso and the local dialect so the dependence on West Indian cultural components sounds correct. The same cannot be said about Naipaul's later works, starting with *The Mimic Men* which mark a change in consciousness, the hatred, the cynicism with which he dismisses what he finds trite, regional and insignificant. The racial issues he touches upon in *Guerrillas* and *A Bend in the River* are irrelevant more to the contemporary national issues and racist posturings than to culture or history. His migration and exile, his life in England and his literary career at the present point of time indicate an exhaustion of his earlier regional, diasporic content that creatively engaged him in negative aesthetics and colonial world view.

V.S. Naipaul is one of the best living English authors in the universe and all his works be it novels, autobiographical writing, travelogues, all are fine pieces of twentieth-century diasporic literature. He is not a pure Indian, not a native Caribbean and not even an English writer. In his writing, he has applied a diasporic culture in raising three identities with him. His writings fall in the following categories—his novels based on Caribbean settings, his books based on foreign locality and his books having the Indian impressions. His Indian impressions are the finest products of his major novels in which he has expressed his diasporic concerns and chosen the matter which creates the finest fictional creations in his novels.

Notes

1. Manjit Inder Singh, *Writers of the Indian Diaspora: V.S. Naipaul.* Second Ed. Jaipur: Rawat Publications, 2002. Print.

2. V.S. Naipaul, *The Enigma of Arrival.* Harmondsworth: Penguin, 1987. Print.
3. V.S. Naipaul, *Finding the Centre.* Harmondsworth: Penguin, 1985. Print.
4. V.S. Naipaul, *The Mimic Men.* London: Andre Deutsch, 1967. Print.
5. *Ibid.*
6. Manjit Inder Singh. *Writers of the Indian Diaspora: V.S. Naipaul.* Second Ed. Jaipur: Rawat Publications, 2002. Print.

7

Vikram Seth's "Homeless" and "Unclaimed": A View through the Diasporic Lenses

Sudhir K. Arora

(I)

> Diaspora: The one who always back looks
> the ones who personify longing. (*Collected Poems* 318)

This is how Keki N. Daruwalla defines what diaspora is. Time and diaspora are interrelated. Place changes and creates distance but time reminds of the former place and connects with it. The moment when man is connected, he looks back and begins to have longing for the place.

(II)

Diaspora, a contested term because of its loose use or overuse, has become crucial in the current postcolonial discourses. 'Being diasporic' or 'charged with diasporic feelings' or 'being conscious of diasporic identity' are the popular postcolonial currencies which are being used in the global market easily. It has become a fashion to use the term even when in the native country a person becomes nostalgic because of alienation. The dispersion of the Jews outside Israel forms 'diaspora' but formally, the word, according to *Cambridge Advanced Learner Dictionary*, means "the spreading of people from one original country to the other countries". Initially, it was used in the sense of exile, a kind of punishment, of which the Old Testament also talks. The very statement: "Thou shall be a diaspora in all kingdoms of the earth" is mentioned in the book of *Deuteronomy*. The agony that a human undergoes when he or she is homeless has been properly represented through the postcolonial writings. Between place and displacement lies in-betweenness. Alienation, longing for roots, a sense of uprootedness and fear, clashes of cultures, identity or sense of belongingness, discrimination, conscious of being peripheral, nostalgia, etc. are some bricks that lay the foundation of the diasporic building.

The diasporic human is like an Indian bride who leaves her home to own her husband's home where she can be happy if she gets love and security of her parental home. The bride becomes unhappy if she misses it. She adopts her new home and adapts herself to the new environment. If circumstances become adverse, she weeps, longing for her parental home. On the other hand, love and security make her forget her original home. Whatever may be the circumstances, she cannot disassociate herself with her parents and other things related with them.

It applies to the people who are either forced to migrate or happily migrate in search of their El Dorado. Migrants never go alone; they may be empty-handed but not empty-minded because they carry with them the traditions and ceremonies which ever remain imprinted on their mindset in the form of socio-cultural baggage. Identity gives a sense of personal belonging which plays a vital role in making decision related with one's way of linking with the people and the world for the purpose of differing or being identical. No doubt, the concept of identity, in the postcolonial context is intrinsic, singular and unitary if it is viewed from the modernist angle but when it is viewed from the postmodernist angle, it is not one but multiple identities that never remain static because of their variable nature.

(III)

"I see myself as Indian and primarily as a poet" are the words which have come from the pen of Vikram Seth (b. 20 June 1952 in Calcutta, now Kolkata), who has passed most of his lifetime while living in England, California, China and India. Currently, he hovers between England and India. Though trained as an economist, he calls himself a poet first and prefers to translate his visions in his poetry. He opines that "For good or ill, one must take one's visions as they come, and be thankful for those that survive" (*The Collected Poems* xv). He writes with ease and rhythm, the characteristics that give musicality to his poems. He makes a flow of tone and movement in his poems without breaking seriousness of content. He says what he has to say but keeps his passions well controlled. The swinging from one place to another place makes him a diasporic poet. Quest for identity, searching for roots and the mesh of being outsider and insider are some of the characteristics which are deciphered in his works, though he likes to call himself an Indian.

(IV)

Vikram Seth likes to recite the poem "Homeless" which is from his poetry collection, titled *The Humble Administrator's Garden*. This poem, somehow, reveals some diasporic ingredients which make the poet longing for the home. Here is quoted the complete poem:

HOMELESS

I envy those
Who have a house of their own
Who can say their feet
Rest on what is theirs alone,
Who do not live on sufferance
In strangers' shells,
As my family has all our life,
And as I probably will.

A place on the earth, untenured,
Soil, grass, brick, air;
To know I will never have to move;
To review the seasons from one lair.
When night comes, to lie down in peace;
To know that I may die as I have slept;
That things will not revert to a stranger's hand;
That those I love may keep what I have kept.
(*The Collected Poems* 112)

(V)

The poet Vikram Seth in the poem "Homeless" recalls his pain and sufferings which he often feels for not having a permanent home. He keeps on oscillating from one place to another. He passed his years sometimes in California, sometimes in China, sometimes in England and sometimes in India. Now he continues shifting from India to England and from England to India. Hence, he envies the people who have a permanent house of their own. He envies the people who live at one place—their native place and do not move from there. He becomes envious of the people who take rest in their own houses as they need not have the feeling of toleration while he himself has to live on sufferance in foreign countries. These are the people who can enjoy and live their lives with their own set parameters while one who lives in the foreign country has to adjust at every step by developing the feeling of toleration. He cries when he sees such people because his own family throughout life had to live in strangers' shells. The poet expresses the possibility of continuity of this process.

The poem "Homeless" raises a question of identity—to which country he belongs to. It reveals his uprooted consciousness which he realizes when he sees the settled people while living in their houses peacefully with their own people among the known customs and traditions. Displacement and alienation are ingredients that make this poem moving—moving to the extent that he begins to search for the roots in the native soil. Due to different assignments, he has to pass a tenured period in several countries. What he wishes is to live at one place for an untenured period. He wishes to associate himself with the very soul of the place that includes soil, grass, brick, air and the like. He is lost in vision which makes him imagine that he has a house from where he will never have to move and so can enjoy all the seasons. He imagines that he may sleep in peace at night and also die at the place where he has slept. But soon he realizes that these things are imaginary for a stranger. They will not come to a stranger's hand. It is not necessary that the people whom he loved may also continue to love him. What he realizes is that his condition is no better than a stranger. This homeless poetic persona may have a house but not a home—the home that may offer him peace within and outside. To counteract this frustration, he seems to have fallen in love with a stranger. Words like 'a house', 'alone', 'stranger's shells', 'untenured', 'one lair', 'peace', 'die', 'sleep', 'revert', 'love' clearly reveal the poet's longing for owning a home which may give him rest and peace as he wishes to be free from the life of shifting from one place to another place. Hence, this poem reveals the poet's mental state of pain and suffering due to displacement and alienation.

(VI)

Vikram Seth's "Unclaimed" like "Homeless" is also from his poetry collection, titled *The Humble Administrator's Garden.* Longing for unclaimed proves his stance of love for the stranger—the diasporic land but this longing somehow reminds him of the claimed one—the native land. Here is quoted the complete poem which can be deciphered from various angles.

UNCLAIMED

To make love with a stranger is the best
There is no riddle and there is no test.

To lie and love, not aching to make sense
Of this night in the mesh of reference.

To touch, unclaimed by fear of imminent day,
And understand, as only strangers may.

To feel the beat of foreign heart to heart
Preferring neither to prolong nor part.

To rest within the unknown arms and know
That this is all there is; that this is so.
(*The Collected Poems* 146)

(VII)

In "Unclaimed", Vikram Seth does not favour for any restrictions, moral compunctions or religious restraints. He criticizes the institution of marriage and family, which bind a man to a circumference, out of which he never comes. Sincere love with promise is out of his dictionary. Permanent relationship does not have any value for him as it longs for devotion from the two partners. What counts for him is freedom. This freedom, the poet believes, cannot be enjoyed in the married life. Love with a stranger is the only fountain that can quench the thirst without encroaching anyone's freedom. Hence, the poet recommends for a free life for the enjoyment of love and sex. He interrogates sex in married life pointing out the restrictions and fear involved in love and sex with the married partner. What he recommends is love and sex with a stranger. 'Claimed versus unclaimed' is the issue that he has raised in the poem "Unclaimed" with his preference for the unclaimed as the unclaimed never approaches for being the claimed. Hence, freedom is secure while pleasure in love and sex is guaranteed with a stranger. Love with a stranger is the best for it offers neither test nor any riddle for the partner. In married life, it is not easy to enjoy as there are many tests which a man has to pass through. Married life itself becomes a riddle. To think of love and sex proves to be a difficult task for the partner because of reluctance, restrictions and moral compunctions.

Even in married life, the partners prefer to go for honeymoon to a place where none knows them so that they may enjoy to their full. What they need is privacy and no restrictions. They wish to run to madness in love and sex without being seen or without being objected or criticized. This is not possible in an Indian society which puts barriers at every step to the road of love and sex. The poet wishes to lie down with a stranger and, then, love her to the extent that he may not feel any aching or fear. He knows that it is not possible with the married partner because there is always a fear—fear of being introduced, fear of being seen, fear of being spoken, fear of being slippery in tongue, fear of being called cynic or freak, fear of talking nonsense, etc. The married partners remain in fear that the night will pass giving place to the day when they will not be able to express love and enjoy sex with each other. He fears that the night will pass while making one reference after another reference, of which there will be no end as he will find himself in the mesh of reference. He will be in hurry for the act of love for the fear of passing of the night—the night that has the fear of imminent day. Hence, the married partner touches his claimed one—wife but fails to enjoy fully for the fear of day while with an unclaimed or a stranger, such fear does not occur. He is neither afraid of passing of the night, nor of any moral compunctions from outside. He attempts to understand the whole situation like a stranger. With a stranger he can feel the beat of foreign heart and she can feel his. This is the time when he prefers neither to make it prolonged nor wishes to part. This is the perfect fusion which he feels with a stranger. Love with the wife in bed is always performed in hurry and so remains without satisfaction. The poet prefers to rest not within the arms of the known but of the unknown and wishes to feel heaven in them. Heaven lies in the unknown arms for there is no claiming after experiencing pleasures. This is the love which is quite free from any kind of responsibility and obligation. The question of promise does not arise as it requires no loyalty. What it needs is love and sex to the utmost satisfaction without being disturbed. As there is no promise or loyalty or moral compunction, the lover does not feel any regret. Repentance remains out of question. When they are separated, they do not claim over each other.

The poet may be right from his perspective. But, in Indian society, if it is applied, there will be chaos. What binds the Indians is the institution of family and marriage. Otherwise, there will be no harmony. To love and have sex with a stranger shatters the very foundation of Indian culture. What he recommends is illicit relationship and complete freedom from all kinds of moral and religious restrictions. If there is no check or restriction, where will the society go? It will give birth to the savage and uncivilized behaviour of the people. It is because of the restrictions and moral compunctions that the Indian culture is alive. The poet is materialistic to the very core and this attitude makes him think body as an object—an object for pleasure. As Indian culture is spiritual to the very core, it takes body not merely an object but a subject—the subject with a soul. This spiritualism postulates sacrifice, devotion, promise and fidelity, faith, love and service.

(VIII)

The poem "Unclaimed" is appreciated for its continuous flow that flows simply through its two separate banks. Unclaimed reminds the reader of claimed. While going through the poem, he comes across the two parallel ideas. No doubt the poet talks of love and sex with a stranger, the reader cannot remain of recalling love and sex of the married couple side by side. Though the poet attempts to be innocent throughout the poem, he is not so. He tries to convince the reader that what he has said is true. With the single idea, the poem runs with rhythm—the rhythm that moves with the rhymes like best-test, sense-reference, day-may, heart-part, and know-so. For convincing the reader, he uses infinitive. He begins his poetic line with 'to' to respond and convince the reader. The use of 'to make', 'to lie', 'to touch', 'to feel', 'to rest' makes the action better, clearer and more dynamic. The use of 'to make love' is not natural; it is not love at first sight. It is the love that is performed knowingly. It does not come out from soul but comes from the bodily touch. Making love with a stranger relaxes him and gives pleasure but not peace or bliss which comes out of the emotional touch—the touch which can be felt only in the married life. Body quenches its thirst but soul remains thirsty. Love without emotional bond is barren. The poet has employed words like 'riddle', 'test', 'mesh of reference', 'fear of imminent day', 'prolong', 'part', etc. to offer the shortcomings that often occur with the married couple. These words emit the negative aroma which convincingly enmeshes the reader. With a stranger, there is no riddle, no test, no mesh of reference, no fear of day, no fear of prolonging and no fear of parting. While the reality is that these are the things that make love everlasting and refreshing. The poet is simple but this simplicity is deceptive as he speaks more than what the words really mean.

(IX)

The poem "Unclaimed" can also be studied from the diasporic angle. Here 'unclaimed' denotes diaspora, which naturally reminds the reader of the claimed 'the native land'. The poet longs for the feel of the beat of foreign heart and this foreign heart gives the feel of diaspora. The poet though hails from India, lives in a foreign country and so loves her. This foreign country where he lives now is the stranger with whom he loves and enjoys sex. Sex is not sex but physical living on the land. He does not wish to prolong this stay nor wishes to part from her. He remains there as he is and is quite satisfied with his present status. He loves to take rest in the unknown arms as he knows that "this is all there is, that this is so". He associates himself physically with the diasporic country. The materialistic light has dazzled him to the extent that he has forgotten the real fountain of light. Body has overpowered his soul. It is India where he finds tests and riddles which stop him from enjoying love and sex without being married. Here with a stranger—in the arms of the diasporic country he lies, he loves and does not ache to make sense. Here he has no fear of cultural values, mores and moral compunctions. What counts him here is pleasure—pleasure of body which, in reality is nothing but an illusion. He loves during night and has no fear of day. He has no mesh of references which he finds in his native country where caring for relationship counts. But here there is no net of relations. Bodily relation is what counts. In India, he finds everyone claiming but here he touches—a stranger, i.e. the diasporic country where there is no fear of being claimed. He attempts to understand this stranger only as a stranger. He knows that when two strangers meet, it will result in association of two bodies, if not of two souls. Somehow, the poet while sharing experiences a stranger—the diasporic country recalls the claimed—the native country on the mental level. The unclaimed, on deconstruction, reveals the claimed. Hence, the poet cannot wipe out the impression of memory of the claimed—the native land. He attempts to bring the unclaimed to the centre from periphery as a reaction to the claimed that remains in the centre in his native land.

(X)

Diaspora is the word which everyone seems to be using it without going into its depth. These days the use of internal diaspora has emerged to the extent that one uses this term if one traces out alienation, loneliness and a sense of uprootedness, fear and clashes of culture. The man suffering from the internal diaspora seems to be at the crossroad which makes him feel neither rooted nor uprooted. He lives somewhere between native and diaspora. Even in his native country, a man may feel diaspora when he comes to the city from the village. The memories of his birthplace make him so nostalgic that he does not feel happy in the city. He feels frustrated as he succeeds in fulfilling his bodily needs but fails to satisfy the need of his soul. C.L. Khatri's poem "A Crane in Cage" beautifully presents the mental state of a man suffering from internal diaspora. He compares him to a crane in cage pointing to his seasonal visit like crane on the peepal tree.

> A crane fluttering in the cage
> questions
> the vertical bars
> jailors
> the roots and the shoots
>
> thinks of ancestral home
> in the archive
> and flies away
> with the cage
> not knowing
> the next stop like a nomad. (*Two Minute Silence* 58)

His condition is no better than a crane in the cage and wherever he goes, the cage remains with him. This cage reminds him of the place and the members associated with it. Though he attempts to forget, he fails. This is what Vikram Seth feels, though he attempts to reveal that he loves the stranger—the unclaimed and is satisfied with his present status. Somewhere, the poet, at the deeper level, suffers from alienation or the failure of communication with the claimed. He wishes to compensate this failure by making love with a stranger. Somewhere riddles, tests, meshes keep on flashing on the screen of his mind. These reminiscences connect him to his roots which he wishes to pluck in one go but fails to do so. Hence, with his intellect he attempts to convince that these bars—tests, riddles are not felt while enjoying love and sex with a stranger. The truth is that the poet in Vikram Seth is a crane that flutters in the cage. He becomes so desperate that he flies away with the cage without knowing that he has the cage with bars which make him lie, love, touch, feel and rest with one stranger after another without having peace of mind, though he claims to feel heaven in the arms of the stranger—the diasporic land. He attempts to fill the gap through communication, which he could not do with the claimed one because of mores, morals, cultural and religious values that prove to be wearisome to his materialistic way of life.

Works Cited

Daruwalla, Keki N. *Collected Poems 1970-2005*. New Delhi: Penguin, 2006. Print.

Khatri, C.L. *Two Minute Silence*. New Delhi: Authorspress, 2014. Print.

Seth, Vikram. *The Collected Poems*. New Delhi: Penguin, 1995. Print.

8

Mapping the Trajectory of Internal Migration: Alka Saraogi's *Kalikatha: Via Bypass*

Gourhari Behera

Diaspora and diasporic writings are significant components of postcolonial studies and in the last few decades have attained cult status in academic circles especially in postcolonial nations. The term 'diaspora' which originally in Greek meant 'to disperse' refers to the "voluntary or forcible movement of peoples from their homelands into new regions" (Ashcroft 68).

Thus, a community can be called diasporic if its members share features like dispersal from an original centre to a foreign country, collective memory, vision or myth about the centre's locations, history and achievements, belief in non-acceptance in the host society, desire to return to the centre when conditioning are conducive, a strong belief in commitment to maintenance or restoration of the homeland. Robin Cohen identifies nine basic features of a diasporic community:

1. Dispersal from an original homeland, often traumatically, to two or more foreign regions.
2. Alternatively, the expansion from a homeland in search of work, in pursuit of trade or to further colonial ambitions.
3. A collective memory and myth about the homeland, including its location, history and achievements.

4. An idealization of the putative ancestral home and a collective commitment to its maintenance, restoration, safety and prosperity, even to its creation.
5. The development of a return movement which gains collective approbation.
6. A strong ethnic group consciousness sustained over a long time and based on a sense of distinctiveness, a common history and the belief in a common fate.
7. A troubled relationship with host societies, suggesting a lack of acceptance at the least or the possibility that another calamity might befall the group.
8. A sense of empathy and solidarity with co-ethnic members in other countries of settlement.
9. The possibility of a distinctive yet creative and enriching life in host countries with a tolerance for pluralism. (Cohen 1996: 515)

Meenakshi Mukherjee while emphasizing the significance of demographic movements in the second half of the twentieth century points out that such migrations "have always been part of Indian history from the undocumented past to the last few centuries of recorded chronicles" (46). For instance, she points out that in the post-1857 period "Bengalis dispersed to many part of North India along with the expansion of the British empire" (46-47) and "Marwari traders and financers from Rajasthan have been moving to different parts of India for the last two or three centuries". The question is: Can these movements, dispersals and exiles be explained in diasporic terms? In other words, Can the insights of diasporic studies especially those of theorists like Stuart Hall, Homi Bhabha, Rey Chow, James Clifford and so on and so forth help in making sense of these movements? Would these movements, much discussed these days in academic circles, automatically qualify for being diasporic?

Mukherjee is of the view that issues of double consciousness, empowerment and celebration which are significant coordinates of diasporic consciousness, according to major postcolonial theorists are insufficient to explain the movements like internal diaspora because "their frame of reference is global, either the earlier diaspora from Africa and China or the more recent diaspora from South Asia to the more developed parts of the world where questions of race and ethnic identity assume importance" (47). So to Mukherjee "these theories can hardly be superimposed on movements within a nation, however large the nation may be territorially" (47).

But for K. Satchidanandan "it may be possible to extend the concept of the 'diaspora' at least in relative, linguistic and regional-cultural terms within the country: the Malayali diaspora in Delhi, the Tamil diaspora in Bangalore, the Bengali diaspora in Bombay, or a Santhali diaspora in Calcutta" (20).

Although Satchidanandan's views have been criticized yet his remarks does bring into focus the problematic of internal diaspora as a category for serious perusal.

The Marwari community has been one of the many migratory communities in India. The Chettinads of Tamil Nadu have also migrated to many parts of the country for various reasons. Even the Gujarati trading classes migrated to Bombay (now Mumbai) in the eighteenth century when maritime activities shifted from Surat to Bombay. After the 'liberation' of Bangladesh, many Bengalis from Bangladesh migrated to India. Should one consider these communities diasporic only on the basis of their dislocation?

If we consider these communities diasporic how do they differ from those who live outside the political boundaries of India? As Vikas Jain in an unpublished article points out, the retaining of "exilic consciousness" by which he means "an attachment to the homeland, return to which may or may not be possible or desirable for various reasons can be the marker of identifying such communities as diasporic. He considers the concept of the 'sub-national diasporas' as a useful category for making sense of such migrations.

Alka Saraogi is one of the most significant of women writers to have emerged in the Hindi literary scene in contemporary times along with Prabha Khetan and Madhu Kankaria. These three writers are Kolkata-based Marwari women who confront issues of identity, belonging gender and class in their works. While Prabha Khetan's *Pilli Andhi* (1996) is the first novel to deal with Marwaris as a migrant community, Saraogi's *Kalikatha: Via Bypass* is path breaking because it can be seen as "a biography of a city, community, country and its little individual passing through centuries" (interview with Avadhesh Kumar Singh. *Indian Literature*, Vol. 50, No. 3, May-June 2006: 166-70).

Alka Saraogi's novel, *Kalikatha: Via Bypass* is an excellent instance of problematizing the notion of internal diaspora in fiction. Saraogi's novel stirred the Hindi literary world to such an extent that it was seen as a revival of the Hindi novel. The novel which centres on the Marwari settlers in Calcutta gives the readers an opportunity to understand the community with a sensitivity that is usually lacking in the assessment of the Marwaris by other communities in India.

The title of the novel is quite significant. Kalikatha simultaneously refers to Calcutta and 'Kaliyuga' and is also about short-cuts because 'by-pass' indicates a surgical procedure, a road diverging from and re-entering a main road and the narrative structure of the book also resembles the various 'by-passes' in the city of Calcutta. And as Meenakshi Mukherjee points out, "Bypass becomes a keyword in the novel by highlighting the short-cuts taken routinely today by which rules can be overlooked to get things done" (51).

Saraogi tries to portray the picture of the Marwaris in Calcutta through the figure of Kishore Babu, a rich Marwari, who after a bypass surgery takes to wandering in the lanes of Calcutta. These wanderings take him back not only to his college days when he was caught between the conflicting ideologies of Subhas Bose and Mahatma Gandhi but also to the distant past when his great-grandfather Rambilas Babu migrated to 'Kalikata' (later Calcutta and now Kolkata) from his native Rajputana when it was struck by famine.

The novel depicts Ram Vilas's struggles, his relationship with the British and Kishore Babu's own struggles—both economic and psychological. Kishore Babu tries answering those questions that he had "by-passed" in his busy and day-to-day life; questions like whether the Marwaris actually betrayed the cause of freedom struggle and independence and helped the British-rule India. Also he ponders over questions like why the Marwaris after leaving Rajputana for far-off places like Bengal were not able to leave Marwar behind mentally.

Saraogi presents the various ways by which the Marwari migrants connect themselves to their "home". Ram Vilas for instance does this by distributing the *prasad* of *ghugri* for twenty-one years in Calcutta at the onset of every monsoon and Vasantlal longs for home because for him living in Calcutta, "a crowded city" is "a punishment".

Also, though Ram Vilas is attracted to the natural beauty of Bengal, he does not have a very high opinion of the host society. Instead he equates them with the British who for him also are "migrants from a distant land" (60).

What is important here is that "exilic consciousness", a significant marker of a diasporic community/individual can be seen clearly in the figure of Ram Vilas and Kishore Babu.

The perception of the members of the other communities towards Kishore Babu in particular and the Marwari community in general is presented in the novel very vividly. Kishore is derogatorily referred to as "Mero" and even his close friend Shantanu, a zealous nationalist, believes that the Marwaris were responsible in the defeat of Siraj-ud-daula at the hands of the British in 1757. Moreover, he also feels uncomfortable about Ram Vilas's association with a British officer named Teggart. He internalizes the negative image of the Marwaris which results in self-alienation. This process of internalizing a derogatory image of oneself based on stereotyping of the "other" by a host community is a characteristic marker of the diasporic or exilic consciousness. Kishore Babu, thus, becomes the emblem of not only the kind marginalization a diasporic community experiences within the host society but also a symbol of self-alienation and self-hatred.

Alka Saraogi's novel expresses the diasporic consciousness of the Marwaris in Calcutta by highlighting the ways the community is subject to the stereotypical gaze of the "host" and other communities resulting in its alienation and self-exile. This consciousness of being the "other" as well as a sense of threat of any man-made calamity is typical to the diasporic consciousness.

Saraogi's attempt at recording the collective history of the Marwari's relationship with the city of Calcutta through the eyes of Kishore Babu brings to the fore the complexities of internal migration. The exilic condition of the Marwari community can safely be termed diasporic as is evident from the study of Saraogi's novel. Thus, *Kalikatha: Via Bypass* engages with and addresses the complex issue of internal diaspora fictionally in order to throw light on a significant concern of our times.

Works Cited

Ashcroft, Bill, Gareth Griffiths and Helen Tiffin. *Post-Colonial Studies: The Key Concepts*. London and New York: Routledge, 2009.

Cohen, Robin. "Diaspora and the Nation-State: From Victims to Challengers", in *International Affair (Royal Institute of International Affairs)*, 1996. 72.3: 507-20.

Jain, Vikas. "Towards a 'Local Diaspora against Dominance of the Global': The Case of Indian Marwaris". Young Researchers Conference, JNU, New Delhi. 17 Jan. 2014. Reading.

Mukherjee, Meenakshi. *Elusive Terrain: Culture and Literary Memory*. New Delhi: OUP, 2008.

Saraogi, Alka. *Kalikatha: Via Bypass*. Trans, Alka Saraogi. Delhi: Rupa Publications, 2001.

Satchidanandan, K. *Authors, Texts, Issues: Essays on Indian Literature*. Delhi: Pencraft International, 2003.

Singh, Avadhesh Kumar. "Alka Saraogi in Conversation with Avadhesh Kumar Singh". *Indian Literature*. Vol. 50, No. 3, May-June 2006: 166-70.

9

Jhumpa Lahiri's *The Namesake*: A Tale of Diasporic Consciousness

Jaba Kusum Singh

In Ancient Greece, the term "diaspora" meant "scattering" and was referred to citizens of a dominant city-state who immigrated to a conquered land with the purpose of colonizing that particular place and people and thereby assimilating the territory into the empire. In the Bible, the word diaspora refers to the population of Jews exiled from Israel by the Babylonians, and again from Judea by the Roman Empire. A chronological study shall confirm that this word came to be used to refer to the historical movements of the dispersed ethnic population of Israel and to the cultural development of that population in an alien land.

The wider application of diaspora evolved from the Assyrian policy of two-way mass deportation of conquered populations to deny future territorial claims on their part. The first known recorded usage of the word diaspora in the English language was in 1876 referring to extensive diaspora work in the preaching of gospel among the National Protestant Churches on the continent. The term became more widely common in English by the mid-1950s, when it was started referring to long-term expatriates in significant numbers from other particular countries or regions. And in academic field, diaspora studies, has become established relating to this sense of the word.

By all means, the term diaspora carries a sense of displacement; that is, they are the people who so described finds itself for whatever reason separated from its native land, carrying deep in their heart a hope, or at least a desire, to return to their homeland at some point; of course if the "homeland" still exists in any meaningful sense. Many writers strongly believe that diaspora may result in a yearning for a single home as people "re-root" in a series of meaningful displacements. And thus it is very important to note that an individual may have multiple homes throughout one's life, with different reasons for maintaining some form of attachment to each. Diasporic cultural development often assumes a different line of conduct from that of the population in the original place of settlement. These aloof and separate communities tend to vary in culture, traditions, language, and other factors. They fight back to retain their last evidence of cultural affiliation in a diaspora and so the community resist to language change and takes pride in the maintenance of traditional religious practice of their homeland.

Jhumpa Lahiri's *The Namesake* is one such novel that celebrates the uniqueness of this urge for home among the diaspora. By now it is clear that theme of rootlessness is too common and variedly dealt by various scholars of diaspora literature and almost every second scholar talks of this feeling of homelessness whenever there is a discussion on diaspora. But when we read the novel of Jhumpa Lahiri, we feel that the author has dealt the theme with the perspective of a woman. The difference lies in its approach and we see that Jhumpa is more concerned with mental diaspora rather than physical. Most of us who all are well acquainted with diaspora literature know that this novel is originally published in *The New Yorker* as a novella and thereafter it was adapted by Meera Nair into a film.

The event of the book moves from Calcutta to New York City to Boston thereby examining the nuances involved in being caught between two otherwise different and conflicting cultures with their highly distinct religious, social and ideological differences. The story revolves around three persons, Ashoke, Ashima and their son Gogol Ganguli. It mainly focuses on their feeling of "to be or not to be" in the words of William Shakespeare. They struggle to establish themselves in a society that they have embraced as their own but the question here is how much they themselves finally embraces the foreign culture and the society where they choose to live. They always find themselves misfit in an alien land. This is truer about Ashima, Gogol's mother who finds herself all alone in the foreign land and in between all mis-appropriateness.

Mis-appropriateness because she finds herself more mentally than physically transported through marriage from hot-humid but colourful and vibrant weather of Calcutta to cold white landscape of New York City. The coldness of the weather overpowers her entire psyche, she struggles to identify herself with the locality, foodings, people but in vain.

The diasporic theme is introduced in the first line of the novel. Jhumpa writes "on a sticky august evening two weeks before her due date, Ashima Ganguli stands in the kitchen of a central square apartment, combining Rise Kris pies & Planters peanuts and chopped red onion in a bowl. She adds salt, lemon juice, thin slices of green chili pepper, wishing there were mustard oil to pore into the mix" (*Namesake* 1). This wish for mustard oil is not a simple wish for appropriate and delicious taste but it underlines her craving for her known surrounding, people and fooding.

The surrounding of her house in New York City seems to her colourless, she feels no warmth around her as if everything is shrouded with colourlessness. Jhumpa's purposeful use of white colour while describing Ashima's residence corresponds with her feeling of lifelessness. She is out of her known society and so she feels lifeless, her just married life is dislocated and colourless and so "there is nothing to comfort her in the off white tiles of the floor, the off white panels of the ceiling, the white sheets tucked tightly into the bed" (4). Colour motif plays an important role, a very strong imagery, used by the author to reflect the mental status of Ashima. She mentally lives in India and her physical existence in America pains her, she is unable to adjust with her unfriendly surroundings.

Ashima tirelessly tries to create her own home by cooking Indian food, Bengali sweet meats and meeting Bengali friends every weekend. Her craving for her motherland is so much so that "nothing has felt normal at all" (5) since she left her country. She consoles herself by reading and re-reading "a tattered copy of *Desh*" (6) a Bengali magazine having a pen-and-ink drawing of her father; for this magazine and her father's drawing gave her the feeling of home. She misses the coziness and the unique indigenousness of the Indian society. She is lonely for like all Indian; she is also used to sharing her sorrows and triumphs with others unlike the Americans who "...in spite of their public declarations of affection, in spite of their miniskirts and bikinis, in spite of their hand-holding on the streets and lying on top of each other on the Cambridge Common, prefer their privacy".

The contrast between the two cultures and societies is beautifully sketched by the author. Ashima remembers how during the marriage ceremony "she was adorned and adjusted by countless aunts, countless cousins hovering around her" (9). But now when she needs it the most, the comfort and love of her dear ones she is lying all alone in the nursing home to give birth to her first child. At this most important juncture of her life, she is left only with her good old memories. She feels tattered between her present and her past; now she is "...far from home, unmonitored and unobserved by those she loved, had made it more miraculous still. But she is terrified to raise a child in a country where she is related to no one, where she knows so little, where life seems so tentative and spare" (6).

This discomfort of Ashima makes her cling more and more to Bengali custom and rituals. She was compelled to follow her husband's path like any devoted Indian wife. When Ashima is pregnant, she feels an ardent urge to be with her dear ones who are missing and found nowhere. On the contrary, she is in a foreign land with unknown people, food, surroundings, climate all around her. She feels isolated and lonely. She becomes sad and morose at the thought of being all alone in spite of having so many loved ones at Calcutta who all must have surrounded her to protect and console her during her labour pain. She also missed the Bengali ceremonies and rituals that are accomplished during the birth of a child. The author, realistically, picturizes the sad feeling of a mother who feels like an alien in an unknown land.

She celebrates Gogol's *annaprasan,* rice ceremony, a Bengali custom of feeding the baby for the first time with rice. She does not miss to call all her Bengali friends in America and cooked typical Bengali foods decking-up the little Gogol in a traditional Bengali style. "Gogol is dressed as an infant Bengali groom, in a pale yellow pajama-punjabi from his grandmother in Calcutta... his tiny forehead has been decorated with considerable struggle with sandalwood paste to form six miniature beige moons floating above his brows. His eyes have been darkened with a touch of kohl" (39).

Ashima is always very particular about maintaining her native tradition. She outrightly rejects the very idea of naming her child after father or grandfather as prevalent in America, in the absence of a suitable name for her new born child. Both husband and wife decide to wait for the letter of Ashima's grandmother bearing the name for their new born baby. It simply sounds ridiculous to them that in America one cannot discharge the baby from the nursing home without naming it. The idea, of naming the baby by their own, without the consultation of the elders of the family, is something unthinkable for the couple.

On the contrary, the hospital staff of New York City finds it blasphemous that the parents can't name their own child. The cultural void is distinct and apparent. The letter with the child's name never reaches America and Ashima's grandmother dies. The missing of the name works as a symbol and it is a powerful imagery projecting Gogol's future. The reader finds that, Gogol is a character who always feels disjointed and fractured between two distinctive different traditions. He finds himself tucked-up in between India and America like the name that got lost somewhere between the two countries.

The author clearly voices the dilemma of all the immigrants who feel homelessness even in their so-called home in a foreign land, for the second generation of the immigrants the crisis of homelessness is more adverse for they grow up with a feeling of an unknowns' at their home itself. The house where they stay with their biological parents is a foreign land to them where the people who resides maintain a completely different lifestyle to which they cannot relate to. These offsprings grow up in a dilemma of what to call their own culture. They are always in confusion. They cannot decide between their surroundings outside their home and inside their home. They find their family culture and their societal norms are absolutely strange to each other.

While grooming the children in a foreign land, the mother of these children faces grave problem. She faces an intricate problem of giving forth a completely different tradition and customs that she finds nowhere in the society outside her own home. These mothers, like Ashima in the novel, try hard, although in vain, to inhibit in their children their ethnicity that their children, though not outrightly, yet silently try to reject and ignore. This indifferent attitude of her own child pains the immigrant mother for whom the child is the only medium she finds to keep her tradition living and vibrant in a foreign land.

Ashima's feeling is of mental homelessness, she never or never can consider America as her home. Her struggle is not only with her outer surroundings but with the growth of her children, Gogol and Sonia, a new front opens up. For the children, America is their home country, their neighbourhood are their own but the home they lived in gave them the feeling of an alien. At home they detested the Bengali ways of living which their parents so religiously followed, especially their mother. Gogol and his sister Sonia enjoyed eating American food unlike their parent and so "in the super market they [his parents] let Gogol fill the cart with items that he and Sonia, but not they, consume: individually wrapped slices of cheese, mayonnaise, tuna fish, hot dogs...at his insistence, she concedes and makes him an American dinner once a week as a treat, Shake 'n Bake chicken or Hamburger Helper prepared with ground lamb" (65). Now the situation is direr she is now face to face with her own offsprings who hated the customs, food, culture and tradition she so religiously clinged to for so many years, in spite of residing in a foreign land. Her home is no more her, for she feels she is living with people who do not appreciate the way of life she so dearly loved and maintained so long. Her diasporic feeling expands and deepens and she feels lonelier.

Her feeling of dispersion get deeper with the passage of time and the more she tries to sting to her indigenous culture the more it seems to loosen its grip from her hold and thus her compulsion to make her son, Gogol, marry a Bengali girl resulted into a massacre as the girl, Moushumi, left her son for her boyfriend Dimitri. The character of Moushumi symbolizes the co-mingling of the customs in a foreign country like America. The American society is a cosmopolitan one where all culture of the world breathes under the same sky and where nobody can maintain their own tradition in its uncontaminated form. Thus, Ashima and her family too witness the warmth of this globosity and her so-called indigenous daughter-in-law rejects her son for a foreign complement.

The urge of Ashima to stick to her own people and tradition is a common urge of all those people living in foreign lands and the author in this novel explores how the ardent push for native land and its traditions constantly haunts and affects the personality of all those living away from their native land.

The question that the fiction puts forth is whether the alienation and dislocation of women like Ashima is just the result of geographical migration or something else, for the world today is converted into a global village where whether one is in her native land or somewhere else she may be alienated anywhere and at any given time. The end of the novel is thoughtful and suggestive.

Although Ashima returns back to Kolkata, India, yet Jhumpa writes, "And though she still does not feel fully at home within these walls on Pemberton Road she knows that this is home nevertheless—the world for which she is responsible, which she has created, which is everywhere around her, needing to be packed up, given away, thrown out bit by bit" (280).

Her re-migration to her homeland from the home she so long lived in America and had made it her own was no less painful. The suggestion here is man needs to understand that change is a continuous process and in this present world it is metaphysical alienation that matters more than social and geographical alienation.

Jhumpa Lahiri being a product of the second generation of migrants fully understands the feelings of a migrated person especially a woman. In the novel, she projects finely, two categories of women, first those who are compelled to migrate as their husband choose to live in a foreign land for economic progress and second comes those who are born in a foreign land like those of Sonia, Ashima's daughter and Meenakshi Ashima's daughter-in-law. Astonishingly enough, Jhumpa shows that both these girls accept the global culture and unlike Ashima they do not sting to their mother tradition and of course marries an American. The suggestion is that it is more important to accept the present rather to live in the bygone days.

On the one hand, the novelist talks of metaphysical alienation and on the other, this novel celebrates the evolution of a cosmopolitan culture that has the capability to accept all customs of the globe. The novel gives a message to embrace the new values and that is the only way to feel at home in a foreign land. It is the woman who has an inherent capability to make a home out of an unknown inhabitant and thus Jhumpa Lahiri through her writing acknowledges the women power that not only accepts and lives with all awkwardness in a foreign land but also tries hard to fight back her left out emotion and the feeling of a scattered individual.

This is the reason why Ashima feels bad to leave America, her present home, where she and her husband had spent most of her life sharing their joys, aspirations and sorrows and returning back to India her homeland that she yearned for so long remains no more so happening an event that she visualized earlier. The fact evolved in this novel is that this is an age of global civilization. The entire globe is a home to the human lot. It is necessary to realize that political, social, cultural and traditional borders are strong and unique in its way but the greatness as a human being is to makeover these borders and identify themselves as a global citizen. Ashima too at the end realizes that her yearning for her homeland was her fascination; for home is where you live with your loved ones.

The novel ends with a suggestion that the migrants must realize that the identity crisis that they are haunted with is not geographical or physical but it is beyond the corporeal; it is ever-widening and never changing. It as widening as the two shores of the ocean that is never visible but that is always there; the need is only to feel that the two shores cannot meet but are always present and are invincible parts of the earth.

Works Cited

Lahiri, Jhumpa. *The Namesake*. New Delhi: Harper Collins, 2003.

Weblink: www.bookrags.com/library/weekly/.../bl-jhumpainterview.htm

10

Diasporic Sensibility in Bharati Mukherjee's *Jasmine*

P.K. Singh

Jasmine (1989) is a revealing story of adventures of Jasmine, the heroine of novel, who begins her odyssey of journey from Punjab to California via Florida, New York and Iowa like a flying bird in search of nest as a rootless traveller. Her search for identity looms loneliness, depression, despair, displacement, identity and existence and her perpetual "widowhood and exile" continues till she emerges as a survivor, a fighter and adapter. Her cultural context to diasporic world is full of crisis of identity and finally her reconciliation to her choice.

In *Jasmine*, Mukherjee tries to unravel the complicated layers of cross-cultural reality through a series of adventures which the heroine undertakes during her odyssey from Punjab to California via Florida, New York and Iowa. Her struggle symbolizes the restless quest of a rootless person expressed by a depressing sense of isolation all around. The story opens with the village astrologer under his banyan tree foretelling Jasmine's "widowhood and exile". It all turns out just as nastily as he says it will, but at the same time, Jasmine is a survivor, a fighter and adapter. Her journey through life leads Jasmine through many transformations—Jyoti, Jasmine, Jase and Jane via divergent geographical locales like Punjab, Florida, New York, Iowa and finally California. Jasmine is a born rebel. At every step, Jasmine revolts against her fate and the path drawn for her. The past is Jyoti's childhood in the small village of Hasnapur, Punjab, her marriage to Prakash Vijh and the consequences leading to her departure to America. The present in her life as Jane in Baden, Iowa where she is a live-in-companion to Bud Ripplemeyer, a small town banker.

Jasmine's transformation from Jyoti to Jane had its own scars and stresses. Jyoti is born in a feudal village of Punjab, eighteen years after the partition riots. The fifth daughter and seventh of nine children of her parents, she is a dowryless, undesirable female child, a curse for them. However, she is bold and intelligent, the first ever likely student of Masterji fit for English education. She is a non-conformist, a rebel who questions the prophecies of the astrologer about her "widowhood and exile" in the harshest terms:

> You're a crazy old man. You don't know what my future holds![1]

This irritates the fortune-teller and he chucks hard on her head and she falls on the ground getting a star-shaped scar on her forehead. This scar is seen as a curse to her but she treats it as her "third eye" and feels like becoming "a sage" (5). She does not believe in the prevalent conviction that "Village girls are like cattle whichever way you lead them, that is the way they will go" (46). To exhibit the force of her belief, she refuses to marry widower selected by her grandmother and eventually ends up marrying Prakash Vijh in a Court of Law.

The cursed and hopeless village girl in Jyoti becomes Jasmine, a city woman, wife of a modern-man Prakash who wishes her "to call him by his first name" (77). This christening means much to her:

> He gave me a new name: Jasmine. He said: "You are small and sweet and heady, my Jasmine. You'll quicken the whole world with your perfume." (77)

After marriage she becomes a true wife in the Indian sense of the term identifying her husband's wishes with those of hers. Prakash's ardent wish was to secure admission in some obscure American institute of technology. They start dreaming about their life in America but as ill-luck would have it Prakash falls a prey to the Khalsa Lions, the rebels demanding a separate land of Khalistan for Sikhs, on the eve of his departure which renders Jasmine heart-broken and alone. A born fighter as she is, she does not allow this heart-rending tragedy to deter her decision. She plans to visit the supposed institute where Prakash had to get admitted and to burn herself a "*Sati*" on the campus of that engineering school. Jasmine's decision leaves her family aghast and they wonder "a village girl, going alone to America without job, husband or papers?" (97).

Jasmine leaves for America on forged papers knowing not what the future holds in store for her. But she is aware of the fate of her likes. She muses:

> We are the outcastes and deportees, strange pilgrims visiting outlandish shrines, landing at the end of tarmacs, ferried in old army trucks where we are roughly handled and taken to roped-of corners of waiting rooms where surly, barely wakened customs guards await their bribe. We are dressed in shreds of national customs, out of season, the witted plumage of intercontinental vagabondage. We ask only one thing: to be allowed to land, to pass through, to continue. (101)

Jasmine is estranged by the uncertainties of her life in an unknown country:

> What country? What continent? We pass through wars through plagues. I am hungry for news, but the discarded papers are in characters or languages I cannot read. (101)

However, she travels to the New World on a Shrimper called "The Gulf Shuttle". Jasmine's first encounter with America is a kind of what Malashri Lal says, "regeneration through violence".[2] The captain of the ship, an ugly fellow, Half-Face who "had lost an eye and ear and most of his cheek in a paddy field in Vietnam" (104) takes her to remote motel of Florida and makes before her indecent proposals. Jasmine requests him that she is a deplorable Hindu widow and her "mission (is) to bring my husband's suit to America" (114), he laughs at her idea: "Getting your ass kicked half way around the world just to burn a suit. I never heard such a fool notion" (114). He remorselessly rapes

Jasmine and this outrage is too much for an Indian widow. He sleeps after promising more sexual excitement later in the night. Jasmine goes to bathroom and decides "to balance her defilement with my (her) death" (117) but before she could do so she discovers that she wants to live. Instantly, she realizes: "I could not let my personal dishonour disrupt my mission." She extends her tongue once slices it, blood oozing—a perfect vengeful image of Goddess Kali out to defy and destroy the 'devil' who has violated her chastity. She kills the demon and for some moment remains perturbed:

> No one to call to, no one to disturb us. Just me and the man who had raped me, the man I had murdered. The room look like a slaughter house. Blood had congealed on my hands, my chin my breasts.... I was in a room with a slain man my body blooded. I was walking death, Death incarnate. (119)

Jasmine's killing of Half-Face is a kind of self-assertion. Her decision to kill herself first is a decision of an Indian woman who lives for her deceased husband as well as the woman of chastity and commitment to wife and husband relationship, but the woman who kills Half-Face is prompted by her self-will to live and to continue her life. "In killing Half-Face", writes Samir Dayal, "she experiences an epistemic violence that is also a life-affirming transformation".[3] Pondering over the agonizing as well as transforming effect of evil, Jasmine says,

> For the first time in my life I understood what evil was about. I was about not being human.... It was a very simple, very clear perception, a moment of truth, the kind of understanding that I have heard comes at the moment of death. (116)

After her violent encounter with the ugly world, Jasmine starts afresh; sans money, sans idea in her surroundings—hungry and thirsty, broken both in body and mind. Incidentally, she happens to meet Lillian Gordon, a kind Quaker lady who harbours her, pities her situation, calls her Jazzy and teaches her to talk, walk and dress like an American. She advises her: "Let the past make you Gordon is committed to help the illegal immigrants." Later on, she encourages Jasmine to proceed to New York for a suitable job with an introductory letter to her daughter staying there. After reaching New York, Jasmine decides to visit her husband's former teacher Devinder Vadhera who has been instrumental in her husband's admission. His home is 'Flushing, Queens' which is part of a Punjabi immigrant ghetto. Vadhera's decision not to come out of their four walls, the "artificially maintained Indianness" (145). Jasmine remembers her five months sojourn at Flushing with pain and despair. "Flushing, with all its immigrant services at hand, frightened me" (145). Again she recalls:

> Flushing was a neighbourhood in Jullandhar. I was spiraling into depression behind the fortress of Punjabiness.... An imaginary brick wall topped with barbed wire cut me off from the past and kept me from breaking into future. I was a prisoner doing unreal time. (148)

Here among the Vadheras she is a helpless widow not entitled to enjoy life. This life is terrifying to her, "I wanted to distance myself from everything Indian, everything Jyoti-like" (145). America has so many surprises for Jasmine in its Pandora's Box. To her dismay, she comes to know that Devinder Vadhera far from being a real professor is a sorter of human hair. This fact unfolds, for the first time, the reality of immigrant life to her and she rationalizes Vadhera's act:

> He needed to work here, but he did not have to like it. He had sealed his heart when he'd left home. His real life was in an unlivable land across Oceans. He was a ghost, hanging on. (153)

This comprehension of reality is further confirmed by the taxi-driver who is a doctor from Kabul and confides to her, "We have to be here living like dogs" (140).

In New York streets Jasmine sees "more greed, more people" (140) like herself. New York seems to be "an archipelago of ghettos seething with aliens" (140). Her failure in understanding the intentions of the American beggar is symbolic of confusion that cries an immigrant in an alien land. She is tossed between a desire for remembering her past and an equally pressing urgency to forget it:

> I feel at time like a stone hurtling through diaphanous mist, unable to grab bold, unable to slow myself, yet unwilling to abandon the ride I'm on. Down and down I go, where I'll stop. God only knows. (139)

The freedom loving spirit of Jasmine finds it difficult to cope with the conservative India represented by the Vadheras and after spending five frustrating months at Flushing one day, she deserts the Vadheras and sets forth for another adventure.

Next we see Jasmine in an apartment on Claremont Avenue, Manhattan with Taylor and Wylie Hayes as a caregiver to their adopted daughter, Duff. This is the best period of her stay in the States. She discovers to her excitement that Taylor is a true professor and at once feels impressed by his humane conduct:

> I fell in love with what he represented to me, a professor who served biscuits to a servant, smiled at her, and admitted her to the broad democracy of his joking. (167)

Taylor gives her a new name "Jase" and she is all excited about her new life with the Hayeses. She recalls, "Duff was my child; Taylor and Wylie were my parents, my family". (165)

In the new surroundings marked by personal warmth, Jasmine becomes more Americanized, more confident of her proficiency in English but her instinctive Indian values do surface now and then. For instance, when she comes to know that Duff is not a natural child but an adopted one, her reactions are culturally revealing:

> I could not imagine a non-genetic child. A child that was not my own, or my husband's, struck me as a monstrous idea. Adoption was as foreign to me as the idea of widow remarriage. (170)

Her Indian sense of values cannot tolerate the sight of "naked bodies combing their hair in front of dresser mirrors" (171). She records her disgust:

> Truly there was no concept of shame in this society. I'd die before a Sob Sister asked me about Half-Face. (171)

She again feels outwitted at Wylie's decision to leave Taylor for economist Stuart in search of "real happiness" (181). She feels defeated:

> America had thrown me again. There was no word I could learn, no one I could consult, to understand what Wylie was saying or why she had done it. (181-82)

It is beyond imagination for Jasmine to think of snapping her bonds with her husband. She comes to realize the "liquidity" and "transitoriness" of human relationships in America. She gets the bitterest lesson:

> In America, nothing lasts, I can say that now and it doesn't shock me but I think it was the hardest lesson of all for me to learn. We arrive so eager to learn, to adjust, to participate, only to find the monuments are plastic, agreements are annulled. Nothing is forever, nothing is so terrible, or so wonderful, that it was not disintegrated. (181)

However, she is not unmindful of the positive side of American ethos. She appreciates the Americans for their democracy of thought and their sense of respect even for those doing insignificant works. The Western civilization has a "Work-Culture" and in this set up everybody is discharging his duty without any complex. She compares her own situation with the Mazbi woman who worked in her house at Hasnapur:

> In Hasnapur the Mazbi woman who'd stoked our hearth or spread our flaking, dried-out adobe walls with watered cow dung had been a maidservant. Wylie made me feel her younger sister. I was family, I was professional. (175)

Jasmine has experienced the best moments of stay in America in the company of Taylor and Duff who are like family for her. Taylor also starts loving her and she too wishes that her role as a "day-mummy" should never end. She is absorbed in the American world forgetting all about her strange mission as she herself accepts:

> Jyoti was now a sati-goddess; she had burned herself in a trash-cum-funeral pyre behind a boarded-up motel in

> Florida. Jasmine lived for future for Vijh and Wife. Jase went to movies and lived for today. (176)

She thinks that she has got an established home and now she will no longer be haunted by rootlessness, "I had landed and was getting rooted" (179) but still her destination is not reached and she is forced to run from New York. She sights the assassin of her husband Sukhwinder, and runs for life to Iowa. But her escape is not a sign of her cowardice, it is 'life-affirming'. "She (Jasmine) is running away for life not escaping from life which is a positive step."[4] Pushpa N. Parekh thinks that Jasmine's stay at Taylor's for two years is the most fruitful period of her life in America:

> This period in Jasmine's life is the most restful and comforting, emotionally and psychologically, intellectually, however, it is a phase of minute observations of complex inner deliberations on, and keen involvement in her new environment.[5]

Again her observations on Taylor-Wylie episode are very minute:

> Wylie's apparent "reasonless" abandoning of Taylor Duff is a jolt back to the inexplicable and unexplainable nature of human action. Instead of fate or destiny or an unknown power being responsible for a family's break-up, Jasmine witnesses an American woman, Wylie, deliberately choosing to leave. Jasmine's inner monologues and silent reflections capture the deliberations on cultural difference and an immigrant woman's emotional adherence to her traditional beliefs while intellectually exploring the new avenues opened to her by the modern value systems.[6]

Jasmine's life in Iowa again begins with her chance meeting with Mother Ripplemayer, the Iowan counterpart of Lillian Gordon. She helps her getting a job in her son Bud's bank as a teller girl and after six months she is the live-in companion of Bud Ripplemayer. It seems that Bharati Mukherjee uses fate and chance as a 'problem-solving-device'. When Jane (Jasmine) meets Bud he is "a tall, fit, fifty-year-old banker husband of Karin, father of Buddy and Vern" (14) but after six months he is a divorcee living with an illegal immigrant:

> Asia had transformed him, made him reckless and emotional. He wanted to make-up for fifty years of "selfishness", as he calls it. (14)

After one year, he is a crippled man living with his Asian wife and adopted son, Du who is a Vietnamese brought from a refugee camp by him. Nobody is safe in violence torn America. Bud falls a victim to one Harlan Kroener who shoots him leaving maimed.

Jane likes Iowa because it is very much like Hasnapur. The farmers here are very much like the farmers of her own village "modest people, never boastful, tactful and courtly in their way" (11). Bud is always uneasy with her past and never enquires of it. To quote Jane:

> My genuine foreignness frightens him. I don't hold that against him. It frightens me too. (26)

It is her strangeness that adds to her beauty:

> Bud courts me because I am alone. I am darkness, mystery, inscrutability. The East plugs me into instant vitality and wisdom. I rejuvenate him simply by being who I am. (200)

Jasmine's every moment is a calculated step into her Americanization and with each development a vital change is marked in her personality. Jasmine's flight to Iowa and her renaming as Jane is indicative of a slow but steady immersion into the mainstream American culture. Here we encounter a changed Jasmine—one who had murdered Half-Face for violating her chastity, now not only willingly embraces the company of an American without marriage but also is carrying his child in her womb. We are simply surprised at her act since every idea revolts at this form of an Indian widow. But one should never forget that she is a rebel who revolts at every step against the path drawn for her. She is an adapter, a survivor. Du is also a fighter who has survived eating worms and rodents in the refugee camp. Jasmine easily identifies herself with Du. "They" communicate silently in a no-questions asked relationship of strong identification: they come from the same

"Third World" and share a common legacy of "suffering and survival".[7]

An immigrant's life is in fact a series of reincarnations. He lives through several lives in a single lifetime. This truth explains the condition of Bharati Mukherjee as well as that of Jasmine. As Mukherjee confides in one of her interviews:

> I have been murdered and reborn at least three times, the very correct young woman I was trained to be, and was very happy being, is very different from the politicized, shrill, civil rights activist. I was in Canada, and from the urgent writer that I have become in the last few years in the United States.[8]

This statement has a marked similarity with Jasmine's outcry:

> There are no harmless, compassionate ways to remark oneself. We murder who we were so, we can rebirth ourselves—in the image of dreams. (29)

Mukherjee, by subjecting her heroine to multiple codes of society and geographical locales seems to send the message that if one has to assimilate oneself to the mainstream culture of the adopted land, one should forget one's past. This notion finds ample support from Jasmine's statement:

> Once we start letting go—let go just one thing, like not wearing our normal clothes, or a turban or not wearing a tika on the forehead—the rest goes on its own down a sinkhole. (29)

Jasmine appears to be a much more strong-willed person. She embarks on her journey to U.S.A. as a typical Indian wife to be a 'Sati' for her husband's cause. But once she realizes her strength and power after murdering her rapist in the very beginning of her journey towards many transformations, she never looks back. Hers is a clear-cut journey towards her being a totally Americanized, self-assured, and self-confident woman. Moreover, going through this process she adopts various identities in the form of being Jasmine, Jase and Jane; proceeding westward both in location and in attitude. She recognizes herself fully, and as a result, decides to accompany her lover "greedy with wants and reckless from hope" (250). Thus, we see that *Jasmine* is full of diasporic sensibility.

Notes

1. Bharati Mukherjee, *Jasmine* (New York: Grove Weidenfeld, 1989), 3.
2. Malashri Lal, "Bharati Mukherjee: The Maximalist Credo" in K.N. Awasthi, ed., *Contemporary Indian English Fiction: An Anthology of Essays* (New Delhi: ABS Publications, 1993), 59.
3. Samir Dayal, "Creating, Preserving, Destroying: Violence in Bharati Mukherjee's *Jasmine*," in Emmanuel S. Nelson, ed., *Bharati Mukherjee: Critical Perspectives* (New York: Garland Publishing, 1993), 71.
4. Jaiwanti Dimri, "From Marriage to Murder: A Comparative Study of Bharati Mukherjee's *Wife* and *Jasmine*," in Suman Bala, ed., *American Literature Today* (New Delhi: Prestige Books, 1994), 173.
5. Pushpa N. Parekh. "Telling her Tale: Narrative Voice and Gender Roles in Bharati Mukherjee's *Jasmine*," in Emmanuel S. Nelson, ed., *Bharati Mukherjee: Critical Perspectives, op. cit.*, 113.
6. *Ibid.*
7. Alpina Sharma Krippling. "Toward an Investigation of the Subaltern in Bharati Mukherjee's *Middleman and Other Stories* and *Jasmine*," in Emmanuel S. Nelson, ed., *Bharati Mukherjee: Critical Perspectives, op. cit.*, 153.
8. Michael Connel, Grearson Jessi and Grimes Tom, "An Interview with Bharati Mukherjee," *Iowa Review,* 20, 3 (1990): 18.

11

Situating Diasporic Identity in V.S. Naipaul's *Half a Life* and *Magic Seeds*

Prakash Chandra Pradhan

Naipaul has dealt with the post-imperialistic situations of individuals who are constantly displaced from their original stands and identities when the values and socio-political realities go on changing quite rapidly. In Naipaul's two novels—*Half a Life* (2001) and *Magic Seeds* (2004)—published in the twenty-first century, the protagonist Willie Chandran goes on searching for his identity in different societies—in India, England, and Africa—which are marred by different kinds of disorder and chaos. Willie, being a rebel, is continuously displaced in a free world without being able to achieve his final identity. He moves on in the different perspectives of history, politics, and culture to explore his identity. In reference to the racial issues of "servile class" and "martial race" there is also emphasis on the aspects of exploitation of the marginalized sections in the society. In a postcolonial/post-imperialistic set up peoples, races, cultures and societies have mobility and better chance of living together and representing each other. To Naipaul, the idea of displacement and continuous change is significant because through a cyclic process of change "decay" is replaced by "regeneration". He therefore considers "ruins" and "destructions" in a positive perspective. Change is important because "imperialism" has been displaced by decolonization and postcolonialism. Naipaul thus thinks that the "idea of flux is positive" as it refreshes a civilization and moves it forward in the path of significant progress. This paper, with reference to *Half a Life* and *Magic Seeds,* argues that the core issue of identity is associated with multiple aspects of a diaspora including his/her homelessness, inheritance, displacement, destabilization and a sense of history.

II

Diaspora has been a dominant feature in life and literature since 1960s. The effective modes of transport, the changing economic and social patterns, epistemological and cultural requirements as well as the uneven growth of technology have brought about globalization in the contemporary world. All these factors have been responsible to initiate diaspora, which has affected lives and works of a number of writers. Diaspora played a significant role in the literary career of V.S. Naipaul too. He was a restless boy in his native place. As an extraordinary child he wanted to escape from Trinidad. After getting an overseas scholarship, he therefore flew to Oxford for higher studies. However, he felt restless soon after he got his degree. His expatriate sensibility motivated him to travel in different countries of the world, but he could not find a place he would settle in and call his "home", although he stayed on in England while he was pursuing his writing career. Having decided to earn his living by writing, he wrote around thirty books of novels, travel writings, short stories (short fictions) and non-fictional prose on the world situations. As a writer, his ambition has been a long chain which cannot be tied to a single post or pillar to remain there. The following remarks by Yashoda Bhat are pertinent in the context of V.S. Naipaul's life and works:

> 'Flights' and 'escapes' are common features in an expatriate's life. The ship and the aeroplane constantly recur in expatriate literature. The expatriate finds in these modes a metaphor for feeling of temporariness, rootlessness, nowhereness, a state of constant mobility and expectancy. (2000: 57)

In expatriate literature displacement, homelessness and incessant travel are dominant features. They are guided by global perspectives rather than by national or regional boundaries. Derek Walcott, a Nobel Prize winning poet, has a convincing argument in this context: "To have loved one horizon is insularity; it blindfolds vision, it narrows experience." True freedom lies in global vision; man becomes the citizen of the world rather than belonging to a particular country. V.S. Naipaul as a writer with such global vision celebrates this idea in his writings. The oppressive rigidities, awkward, outdated traditions, creative sterility, stagnation and irrelevant rituals do not confine an expatriate when he is away from his homeland. He becomes unprejudiced while judging the jaundiced outlook of the natives of his homeland. Exile, voluntary or imposed, brings out creative freshness in a writer. However, migration of an expatriate from the margin to the centre is also replete with multiple problems. One such dominant aspect faced by him is "identity crisis". The euphoria of his dreams lasts only for a short while. That is because of his cross-cultural existence. This cultural alienation may be cross-racial, cross-ethnic, cross-religious or cross-lingual. The diasporic trends in Naipaul's writings predominate. In all his books, the theme of cultural alienation, assimilation and acculturation has been an important aspect. He has woven his various moods as a diaspora into his writings. Sometimes, the writer confronts the two ways of life in his homeland and the vast country resulting in his depression. The mood of nostalgia is a significant surrogate in the diasporic writer. Such an aspect in Naipaul is very strong for which he repeatedly refers to Trinidad and India in his writings. The expatriate writings of Naipaul therefore tend to be tools in aid of awareness and rediscovery of *Patria*. *Patria* seems to be an inescapable power, and "expatriacy an indeterminate state". The bond between the writer and his homeland is a source of creativity and joy for the writer.

To V.S. Naipaul, both Trinidad and India are his homelands—Trinidad being his place of birth and India being the place of birth of his ancestors. Though Naipaul has often criticized India and Trinidad in his writings, his creative strength is actually based on his displacement, identity crisis, homelessness and his sense of being "marginalized" in England. An expatriate writer has a complex existence and a complex personality. At times, he may appear to be a bundle of paradoxes because of his paradoxical statements. The basis of such conflicting statements may lie in the fractured sensibility of the expatriate writer. Analysing the writer's dilemma, Sudha Rai observes that Naipaul responds both as an Indian in India, and a Westerner in India: "Naipaul's joy and exultation come from his former self. His flight from India punctuated by his brief returns—the patterns of venture and withdrawal express perfectly the dilemma of the expatriate self" (1982: 27). Even though expatriatism is at times complex, paradoxical and baffling, it has still some positive aspects. Bhat therefore remarks:

> The process of acculturation and self-actualization portrayed in expatriate literature can transform the status of self-alienation into attitudinal changes both in the majority and minority cultures. The expatriate, with his complexities, paradoxes and nostalgia gradually becomes acceptable in the foreign country and the foreign country itself becomes more receptive and assimilative. Such is the total process of globalization and the expatriates' complex life is the mechanics of its actualization. (2000: 63)

Like other famous writers from West Indies such as Derek Walcott, George Lamming and Wilson Harris, expatriacy has always been in the background to push Naipaul forward to achieve his goal. Like some expatriate Indian writers such as Bharati Mukherjee, R. Parthasarathy, A.K. Ramanujan and many others, Naipaul has been mostly haunted by his imaginary homelands—both Trinidad and India. Such imaginary-preoccupation has helped his expatriate sensibility to indulge in reconstruction of his homelands. The loss of "home" and "identity" with which he has struggled significantly, is very powerful in Naipaul. The physical and geographical reclamation of the homeland has been substituted by the imaginary and fictional one. Salman Rushdie, himself an expatriate writer, pleads that exile or emigrant writers are rather haunted by a sense of loss and reclamation of the homeland. They can never reclaim their homeland physically. These writers therefore create "fictions, not actual cities or villages, but invisible ones, imaginary homelands, Indias of the mind" (Rushdie 1992: 10). In real terms, an expatriate writer gains more than what he loses. It is a great compensation. His production of literature has been a huge effort in enriching expatriate literature. Naipaul is one such genius in this field of literature. This paper is thus an attempt to discuss the diasporic concerns of Willie Chandran the protagonist, through his continuous displacement and identity crisis because of leading a life of destabilization in Naipaul's last two novels, namely *Half a Life* and *Magic Seeds*. These two twenty-first century novels share some of the important autobiographical and diasporic concerns of the author himself.

Horace Engdahl, delivering the presentation speech for the 2001 Nobel Prize in literature at the Stockholm Concert Hall, compliments Naipaul for his distinctive way of presenting experience with non-attachment: "Sir Vidia! Your life as a writer calls to mind what Alfred Nobel said to himself: 'my homeland is where I work, and I work everywhere'. In every place, you have remained yourself, faithful to your instinct. Your books trace the outline of an individual quest of unusual dimensions. Like a Nemo piloting a craft of your design, without representing anyone or anything, you have manifested the independence of literature" (Ray 2005: xvi). In reply to the award, Naipaul in his "Nobel Lecture" titled "Two Worlds" said that everything of value about him was in his books (*Literary Occasions* 2004: 181). Elaborating this idea he says: "Each book intuitively sensed and in the case of fiction, intuitively worked out, stands on what has gone before and grows out of it. I feel that at any stage of my literary career it could have been said that the last book contained all the others. It's been like this because of my background. My background is at once exceedingly simple and exceedingly confused" (*LO* 183). He further clarifies: "In Trinidad, bright boy though I was, I was surrounded by areas of darkness. School elucidated nothing for me, I was crammed with facts and formulas. Everything had to be learnt by heart; everything was abstract for me" (*LO* 190). After he became a writer, "those areas of darkness as a child" always haunted him. He therefore becomes nostalgic, and elaborates:

> The land; the aborigines; the New World; the colony; the history; India; the Muslim World, to which I also felt myself related; Africa; and then England where I was

> doing my writing. That was what I meant when I said that my books stand one on the other, and that I am the sum of my books. That was what I meant when I said that my background, the source and prompting of my work, was at once exceedingly simple and exceedingly complicated. You will have seen how simple it was in the country town of Chaguanas. And I think you will understand how complicated it was for me as a writer. (*LO* 190)

Concluding his Nobel Lecture, Naipaul says that every book has amazed him because he has been able to handle the "baffling" nature of his material through his "intuition". Referring to Proust's book *Against Sainte-Beuve,* Naipaul believes that a little "luck and labour" could enable a writer to create beautiful things by capturing "the blurred memories" and "transforming them into his world of creation" (*LO* 195).

A writer's vision in his art should be understood in the perspective of his biography, contemporary situations and convictions. However, the writer as a "social man" is quite different from the writer as an "artist" who is doing his work in "seclusion". The deepest conviction comes to the artist when he is engaged with his works with full concentration: free from the world outside it. Even then, the background, his experiences on different occasions come to him indirectly whenever he is deeply engrossed in his work. Naipaul believes that the details about the life of a writer may give us some impressions, "but the mystery of the writing will remain. No amount of documentation however fascinating, can take us there. The biography of a writer—or even the autobiography—will always have this incompleteness" (*LO* 182). The "new historical approach" stresses on interpreting literary texts from the perspective of their historical and cultural conditions of productions. In the context of a recent new historical approach to Lawrence's works it has been viewed rightly:

> Lawrence's "letters" hitherto regarded as "marginal" can be studied as "central" to his ideas and visions in the context of his major cultural products, the novels. By that way, there will be constant and continuous interactions between the events of his life, his contemporary history

> and culture as well as his concepts and visions. Such an approach in the context of ideologies of our era will reveal many areas of meaning in Lawrence hitherto escaped our notice. This will also enable us to bring out the current relevance of Lawrence's ideas and vision in the context of our own culture and social set-up. (Pradhan 2009: 3-4)

New historical approach to literary study, propounded by Greenblatt and others, argues for a dialectical relationship between past and present and rejects the concept of history as a record of the past event. Such an approach deconstructs the notion of "history as context" because the text should be understood as "a privileged moment within a network of discursive and material practices". Greenblatt also argues that the "historical situation" as well as "intentions and genre" are important for understanding a text because all are social and ideological. He therefore pleads: "And in response to the art of the past we inevitably register, whether we wish to or not, the shifts in value and interest that are produced in the struggles of social and political life" (1990: 112). The creator of the text therefore cannot be disconnected; he is a "connected personality" with his life, past and present altogether. He is "simultaneously historical, political and cultural". In this context Greenblatt's argument is quite convincing when he says that "a work of art is the product of a negotiation between a creator or class of creators, equipped with a complex communally shared repertoire of connections and the institutions and practices of societies" (1990: 158). Though Naipaul thinks that biography and autobiography can never fully reveal the source of the books of the writer. Patrick French, his biographer however views that "the best writing can be examined only in its effect. Sometimes, a critic or biographer can see the things the author cannot". He is right when he says that an individual is so complicated that it is difficult to bring out a parallel between the incidents of a writer's life and the key ideas in his literary texts. He therefore views that "the best a biographer can hope for is to illuminate aspects of a life and seek to give glimpses of the subject, and that way tell a story" (2008: xviii). In the essay "Conrad's Darkness and Mine" Naipaul says: "To understand Conrad, then, it was necessary to match his experience" (*LO* 2004: 171). He also pleads that "every great writer is produced by a series of special circumstances" (*LO* 173). All the circumstances of the writer are to be considered deeply. The most imaginative writers, Naipaul believes, discover themselves through their work. In that essay Naipaul elaborates: "To take an interest in a writer's work is, for me, to take an interest in his life. One interest follows automatically on the other" (*LO* 174). Experience of a writer is therefore very important to mould his visions and ideas. It is the foundation of his basic assumptions and thoughts. To Naipaul, "the myths of the great writers usually have to do with their work rather than their lives". He argues that the work is more important than the writer. Writing about the purpose of the novel, Naipaul argues that the novel must contain convictions rather than experimentation. Naipaul's ideas of the world in writing more specifically in a novel should be related to the world which is new every moment. He therefore argues that the novelist should involve himself in his interpretive function of the "new world" which is changing every moment. To the question of the secretary to the Nobel if he would accept the Nobel Prize, Naipaul said that the Nobel was "a great tribute to both England, my home, and India, the home of my ancestors" (French 2008: xii). In the context of his insult to his homeland Trinidad, French writes: "Creating tension, insulting his friends, family, or whole communities left him in excellent spirits" (xiii). French further comments on the attitude of Naipaul in rejecting his homeland:

> Naipaul's dismissal of his own homeland became part of his persona, a persona he invented in order to realise his early ambition to escape the periphery for the centre, to leave the powerless for the powerful and to make himself a great writer. I sometimes thought of him as a man running up a beach with the advancing tide behind him managing to stay a bare step ahead of the water. In order to become what he wanted to be, he had to make himself someone else. He could not remain regional. (2008: xv)

In spite of the fact that Naipaul viewed differently, a perspective of his life—his frustrations and anxieties, his notions and assumptions, his formulations and constructions about the world at different stages of his life—is essential for us to understand visions and ideas in his works including the most recent novels interpreted in this paper.

III

Naipaul vividly portrays postcolonial societies where sufferings of marginalized people are prominent. However, some of the protagonists, thrust with so many challenges, try to overcome the difficulties and establish their identities. The sense of history and imperialism, domination-dominated dichotomy has always been in Naipaul's psyche as an individual or as a writer. In *A Way in the World,* Naipaul throws light on the situations of the postcolonial world in relation to the colonial history. In *Half a Life* (2001), the writer portrays the character, Willie, who is put to live in alien places, and searches for his identity Willie Somerset Chandran is born in India, moves to London, lives a Bohemian life, publishes a book, and marries Ana, a woman of mixed African descent and then moves with her to Africa to her family estate.

Willie is split in himself because he is unable to reconcile to his father's marriage to an untouchable, though he is a Brahman. Even in Africa, he has a sense of "homelessness", and therefore leaves it for search of his true identity because he thinks he has only lived a half life, a shadow life. The novel has an open-ending because Willie's search for his existence continues endlessly, and we do not know what happens to him as a rebel. The next novel by V.S. Naipaul is *Magic Seeds* which reconstructs the Indian belief-system inherited from the British Empire. The Indians have been made to believe throughout history that "in India there were servile races, people born to be slaves, and there were martial races" (*MAS* 10). This notion of British Empire has been outright rejected by Sarojini, Willie's sister, who believes that such false belief system has been an imperialistic idea of the British. She understands that the so-called martial races have been abused by the British for their ulterior motives whereas "some servants" have often exhibited courage to fight for justice against the oppressors. This is very much central to the thematic structure of this novel. This postcolonial notion deconstructs the idea of "servile" class and "martial race" with reference to history. It is therefore important to study Naipaul's later novels in the context of racial issues, suppression of histories, search for roots, the displacement, and oppression of the marginalized people. In the following pages, we will analyze and interpret the last two novels to touch upon Naipaul's concerns for oppression, and his desire for liberation of these oppressed people who are rather rootless and marginalized in a world of continuous change and destabilization.

Half a Life (2001)

The theme of exile is central to the novel *Half a Life*. The central idea of the novel revolves around the protagonist Willie Somerset Chandran, born in India in the 1930s, moves to Nottingham for study, remains in a state of tension, publishes a book, marries Ana, a woman of mixed African parents, and then goes along with her to Africa, her family estate. Willie is not in a stable frame of mind and questions his own background. His father is a Brahmin who has married an "untouchable" woman and lives in a monastery. Willie does not like such a haphazard life of his father although he leads a life which tallies with the life of his father more or less. Even if he lives in Africa with his wife, he does not feel Africa as his home, and therefore he is an outsider there. That is why after eighteen years he divorces her and tries to explore his existential identity. In Africa, he has led a half-life, an unreal shadow life. The ending of the novel is rather exploratory in the context of Willie's realization that he has led a meaningless, futile life in his wife's native country, Africa: "But now the best part of my life has gone, and Eve done nothing.... And even if we go to Portugal, even if they let me in there, it would still be your life. I have been hiding for too long" (*HL* 227). Ana's reaction to Willie's realization of living a "Half Life" is worth-mentioning. Ana tells him: "Perhaps it wasn't really my life either" (*HL* 227). Actually nobody leads a full life. Even at the beginning of the novel, Willie questions his father, "Why is my middle name Somerset?" (*HL* 1). This is an existential question which is related to the identity of Willie. From the very beginning Willie is disturbed about his identity. Perhaps Willie's father himself while giving Somerset's name to his son, is a split personality as he mixes up illusions and reality. Willie's father is not only leading a half life himself, but creates a background to the dilemma of his son leading a half life throughout. In this context, Asha Choubey comments: "This question forms the very essence of a person's existence. The answer to this question brings into light the irony of Willie's existence and at the same time prepares the background of his half-life in half-made societies with people who are themselves leading their lives which are "half-discovered, half-realized and half-lived" (2002: 1).

In this novel, Naipaul presents the anguish and predicament of "unanchored souls" (Nandan 2000: 56). Willie's predicament is that he does not know himself well initially. He tries to explore his own self to know his identity. In India or London or Africa he is always the half-man and therefore leads a half-life only. The book is therefore about the half lives of various people: "In a larger sense the novel points to various predicaments of various half-and-half people and of people uprooted from a way of life on account of factors often out of their own control. A war, an uprising, a change of government, ethnic hostilities that make people feel threatened, caste considerations are some of those factors. The book also suggests that most of us get only 'half a life'...to live choices of various kinds that we make do shut out other ways of life to us" (Sharma 2007: 176-77). It is true that the protagonist of the novel, a man uprooted from his home and ancestry, is facing a crisis of identity. Even other characters in the novel are also swayed by this social chaos: "*Half a Life* continues the existential search of Willie in particular and other characters in general. Percy, Marcus, Rozer, Ricardo, Carla, Graca, Correias, Alvaro, and Noronha are all searching for meaning in their lives. The social chaos in the form of wars is the hostile condition, which invigorates them. The search for their identity paves the way to their self-discovery" (Mishra, *ACR*, 3.2, 2004: 134-35). The postcolonial linkage to *Half a Life* can also be considered from the point of view of Willie being portrayed as a postcolonial intellectual writer. Willie being a postcolonial migrant has a deeper understanding of the cultural life of London as well as of Africa than the natives of these places: "The experiences he (Willie) received in London remained within him as latent properties which are compared with his experiences in Africa and then the "codes" received in London are "translated" in Africa. The existential suffering of the exile that Willie had to undergo in the multiracial society of the Portuguese Africa prepared him to assert his individuality" (Haldar 2005: 246).

After listening the story of "wretchedness" and "self-disgust" of his father. Willie expressed his hatred towards him: "I despise you...what is there for me in what you have said? You offer me nothing" (*HL* 35). However, Chandran would argue: "It has been a life of sacrifice. I have no riches to offer you. All I have are my friendships. That is my treasure" (*HL* 36). In the context of Sarojini, Chandran said to his son: "Her prospects in this country are not bright. But foreigners have their own ideas of beauty and certain other things, and all I can hope for Sarojini is an international marriage" (*HL* 36). In the first chapter, the novel focuses on the life of Chandran, who actually goes through a series of upheavals in search of identity. In an effort to break with the ancestry through his insistence on marrying a *dalit* woman by following the ideals set by the Mahatma during the pre-independence period. Chandran had an obsession to be a great man like him. His compelled life of spirituality gave him an identity, which his son now challenges. His grandfather's lineage to the temple life shows us that the man was to undergo starvation till he broke with it to become a letter writer outside the Maharaja's palace. Chandran's father, who continued as a courtier of the Maharaja, was however obsessed with the temple cult. Chandran, who understood his grandfather's rage against the poverty of the Brahmins by sticking to their ancestral profession, wanted to do something by which he could be a free man and live with dignity. Though he studied in the Maharaja's college, he was however disillusioned to learn the stereotyped, mechanical way of learning. That is why he found no interest in learning the romantic poets and other renowned writers who told only lies according to his own observations. He therefore wanted to do something greater for which he burnt his books as a mark of protest against the English education in India. Later on when he joined the service in the Maharaja's Tax Department, he was also frightened to think of leading such a life of servility to work in the office throughout his life. It was very much frightening on his part for which he was not working like others. He did not want to marry the Principal's daughter for which the charges of corruption were framed against him. Finally, he led a life of sacrifice under confusion, compulsion and disillusion.

Though he could establish his identity as a '"spiritual man", later on Chandran was rather disillusioned to see that Willie, his son was drifting away from his ideals. In the beginning of the second chapter, there is also a reference to both the identities of Chandran and Willie in the question of the Canadian teacher in the mission school: "What does your father do?" (*HL* 37). The strange reply of Willie with irritation is also interesting to note: "You all know what my father does" (*HL* 37). In the mission school where their mother had been a student, Willie and Sarojini studied. But it was a branded school where backward caste children also read. It was noteworthy that Willie was doing excellent in the composition class by composing stories of inventive nature. However, the father noted that Willie invented stories of lies like Shelley, Wordsworth and others. He thought about his son:

> He is not me. He is his mother's son. All this mom-and-pop business comes from her. She can't help it. It's her background. She has these mission school ambitions. Perhaps after a few hundred rebirths she will be more evolved. But she can't wait like other decent folk. Like so many backwards nowadays, she wants to jump the gum. (*HL* 41)

A week later when Chandran again went through the exercise book of his son, he found another offensive composition against mom and pop. He therefore thought that the boy, the "true son of his mother, was challenging him, with all the slyness of a backward, and he wasn't sure what he should do" (*HL* 41). Remembering the Mahatma's "Civil disobedience", he did nothing to the exercise book. Willie, back from school, thought about his father: "Not only is he a fraud but he is also a coward"

(*HL* 41). During his crisis Chandran was practicing this "vow of silence". However, two or three weeks later he was to break the silence due to a breakdown of Willie after seeing a picture of a priest with glasses and a wristwatch standing with one foot on a statue of the Buddha. Willie had decided not to go to school, nor even to Canada to become a missionary. Chandran was moved to see his son one day sleeping with his face down with the closed copy of the school edition of *The Vicar of Wakefield*:

> There was such unhappiness and such energy there that he was overwhelmed with pity. He thought, 'I used to think that you were me and I was worried at what I had done to you. But now I know that you are not me. What is in my head is not yours. You are somebody else, somebody I don't know, and I worry for you because you are launched on a journey I know nothing of'. (*HL* 49)

This realization of his father was a great compliment to his son. To his father Willie was meant for a special purpose. He therefore wrote to the contact persons abroad whom he had helped in India to arrange a place for his son in some institute. But it was not that easy. Many letters came with no concrete help. Finally, there was a positive response from a famous man from London who had paid a brief visit to the *ashram* just after independence. This letter created an opportunity for Willie to go to London. It was his father's gift. But then, Willie's father did not know concretely about the mysterious journey of his son. He did not know what his son's destiny was, what his identity would be. Even Willie, a boy of twenty did not know what his London life would bring for him in future:

> And that was now, when he was twenty, Willie Chandran, the mission-school student who had not completed his education, with no idea of what he wanted to do, except to get away from what he knew, and yet with very little idea of what lay outside what he knew, only with the fantasies of the Hollywood films of the thirties and forties that he had seen at the mission school, went to London. (*HL* 51)

In his early London days, he would realize his ignorance, and therefore he read a number of books on world history and politics. He could not understand many of them. Meeting many people he would realize the hardships of a real life. He would therefore admire his father's ability: "I misjudged my father. I used to think that the world was easy for him as a Brahmin and that he became a fraud out of idleness. Now I began to understand how hard the world must have been for him" (*HL* 58). Willie knew a lot of rules to cope with the college as well as London life. At the end of his second-term, he saw clearly that the old rules no longer bound him. He therefore wanted to write his own revolution: "The possibilities were dizzying. He could within reason, re-make himself and his past and his ancestry" (*HL* 60). He reconstructed his identity through his father's connection to the greater writer and the journalist, his mother's uncle as a kind of "trade union leader, a pioneer of workers' rights"; his mother as "belonging to an ancient Christian community of the subcontinent, or a community almost as old as Christianity itself", and his father a Brahmin, his grandfather as 'a courtier' and so on (*HL* 60-61). In this way, Willie remade himself which gave him a feeling of power. This seemed that Willie was settling down in London. With some confidence Willie moved on in London, first making friendship with Percy Cato, a Jamaican of mixed parentage. Willie now realized that it was necessary for everybody to establish his identity in the world. Through Percy, Willie was being introduced to the "special, passing bohemian immigrant life of London of the late 1950s" (*HL* 72). A number of immigrants from the Caribbean, the white colonies of Africa and Asia along with some English people were also exotic to have a taste of social adventure, "a wish from time to time to break out of England and people with colonial connections who wished in London to invert the social code of the colonies" (*HL* 72). Willie led a bohemian life of the writers in London along with such friends as Percy, Roger, Richard, Perdita and so on. Roger, a lawyer, suggested Willie to write stories not necessarily having a neat beginning and a neat ending because life in reality is not like that: "Life doesn't have a neat beginning and a tidy end. Life is always going on. You should begin in the middle and end in the middle and it should all be there" (*HL* 83).

Willie, accepting the suggestion of Roger, revised his early stories of the missionary school days, and then wrote some more stories for finding a publisher for them. He was anxious for the publication of the book. Finally Richard agreed to publish it. The book had India as a background setting. Through the book he wanted to have an identity. However, his book could not be reviewed much favorably. Willie was gradually being fed up with those bohemian parties with Percy and June and others. In the meanwhile, he was informed about the international marriage of Sarojini with a German in Berlin. Now Willie could learn in London that "Everything goes on a bias. The world should stop, but it goes on" (*HL* 113). Without getting so much favorable reviews of the book, Willie was a little frustrated: "Let the book die. Let it fade away. Let me not be reminded of it. I will write no more. This book was not something I should have done, anyway. It was artificial and false. Let me be grateful that none of the reviews spotted the way it was done" (*HL* 123). Richard's catalogue contained a half page somewhere in the middle. It was rather depressing because it presented Willie as "a subversive new voice from the subcontinent and the stories having a universal Indian Provincial setting: "The catalogue entry, modes, even bleak commercially self-denying, seemed less a tribute to the book than a tribute to Richard and the well-known politics of his firm" (*HL* 122). Willie felt that his book was now "tainted" and "dead". However, Willie got two letters of compliments for the book from Roger, his friend and Ana, a young woman from an African country. To Willie, the letter from Roger seemed to be "cool and distant". The other letter from the Portuguese-sending name, who was doing a course in London, contained some positive remarks about the book: "I feel I had to write to you because in your story for the first time I find moments that are like moments in my own life, though the background and material are so different. It does my heart a lot of good to think that out there all these years there was someone thinking and feeling like me" (*HL* 124). When Ana came to meet him in the college, Willie could understand that for the first time in his life he met someone who accepted him completely. At home in India, his life was governed by mixed inheritance, rules and regulations. In England, he lived with the idea of difference to be liberated from the cruelties and rules of home. At this point of time Willie received a letter from Sarojini, his sister from Cuba enquiring about his plans for future and the publication of his book: "Was your book published? You kept it to yourself. You didn't send us a copy: and I suppose it's come and gone. Well, now that you've got it out of your system, it's time for you to put that kind of vanity aside, and think more constructively about the future" (*HL* 130).

But Willie had not planned anything for his future. He had been living in a fool's paradise. His time was going to be over in the college. It was time for him to get a job and a place to live in with Ana. After much contemplation he realized that he would have to go to Ana to Africa where they could live together. After such a proposal Ana. though agreed, told him: "Let's see how you like the bush. We need a man on the estate. But you have to learn the language" (*HL* 131). It was significant to understand the views of Sarojini to her brother in her last letter before Willie left for Africa: "Outsiders who go to India have no idea of the country even when they are there, and I am sure the same is true of Africa. Please be careful. You are putting yourself in the hands of strangers. You think you know what you are going to but you don't know all of it" (*HL* 131). These words of his sister that represented mimicking adulthood had no much impact on him. He rather took it differently: "She likes her own international marriage, but she is worried about mine" (*HL* 131). Thereafter he undid the centre of his London life, he started himself with Ana to African city, he did not know. Africa was a strange country with its strange people and strange language. Initially, he thought of staying in Africa for a few nights only and then he would leave the place. After reaching Ana's estate house Willie was disturbed seriously: "I don't know where I am. I don't think I can pick my way back. I don't ever want this view to become familiar. I must not unpack. I must never behave as though I am staying" (*HL* 135). However, Willie spent eighteen years in Africa with Ana. After he shipped one day, he was injured for which he was to be treated in the military hospital among the wounded black soldiers. Willie expressed his desire to leave Ana in the hospital itself. However, Ana consoled him and told him: "People exaggerate the fighting in the bush. You know that. There's not going to be a new war" (*HL* 135). Such a hopeful consolation did not have any effect because Willie did not think about the war, he rather thought about the world, which is full of slippery substances. It is important to understand the mindset of Willie after his shadow life in Africa for long eighteen years. It was a life he desired without knowing its consequences. Now after experiencing it, he thinks that his life has become meaningless. Then he decided to go away to some unknown destination again without knowledge of its consequences. The following dialogue elucidates the idea well:

> When she came back, he said, "Do you think it would be possible for someone to look at all my bruises and cuts and work out what had happened to me? Work out what I have done to myself?"
>
> "You're recovering your spirits."
>
> "You've had eighteen years of me."
>
> "You really mean that you are tired of me."
>
> "I mean I've given you eighteen years. I can't give you any more. I can't live your life any more.
>
> I want to live my own."
>
> "It was your idea, Willie. And if you leave, where will you go?"
>
> "I don't know. But I must stop living your life here."
>
> (*HL* 136)

Willie's unknown destination was Berlin. Reaching there he told his sister about his life in Africa in the manner his father had told him about his story in India. Willie was a rootless man throughout his life. When he was in India, he was too much restless, and when he came to London, he still felt that he was unsettled although his tutors felt that he seemed to settle. In Africa, he led a very adventurous life of a diaspora without being settled though once Ana, his wife commented that he was settling there. Coming Berlin he saw that Tamil boys, displaced and uprooted, were raising funds for a war. His friend, Percy went back to Jamaica, his native land. He himself returned to his sister in Berlin after spending eighteen years, the best part of his life. He didn't know how to move on and where to go in future. This postcolonial dilemma of Willie is reflected in his thoughts by seeing the Tamil boys in Berlin. Willie's experience of postcolonial Africa is illuminating. Without knowing anything about this colonial country—its people, its racial tension, strange manners and situations—he went there because he loved Ana and lived on with her with belief on her luck. Willie needed Ana for his idea of himself being a man. He depended on her strength and authority to be secured, to lead a comfortable life: "She was a woman who had given herself to me. I believed that she was in some essential way guided and protected, and as long as I was with her no harm could come to me. It may be because of something in our culture that, in spite of appearance, men are really looking for women to lean on" (*HL* 141). For one year Willie was quite exciting about his new life in Africa. He enjoyed substantially by meeting new people and the excitement of the Africans in a postcolonial world. Ana's authority on the estate helped a lot in removing people's doubts about Willie. But then after a year or so he began to understand the truth: "I was helped in this understanding by my own background—that the world I had entered was only a half-and-half world, that many of the people who were our friends considered themselves, deep down, people of the second rank. They were not fully Portuguese, and that was where their own ambition lay" (*HL* 160-61).

Africa is a strange country with strange attitude of the people about their security there. The Correias, proud of their aristocratic names, lived with the idea of great disaster about to happen when they would lose their security both in Portugal and Africa for which they had bank accounts in New York, London and Switzerland so that when that disaster came, they could move easily to these places with a good sum of money. This was their idea of security in Africa, a place of half-life even for them. The way of life changes in seconds. There was certain uprising in a region in Africa in the third year of Willie's stay there for which people must learn shooting with a gun as the government would increase the strength of garrison. Willie was therefore to undertake this shooting work on Ana's Estate: "In a second the scale of things could alter and I could be lost in something like private universe. It was strange being on the shooting range in Africa and thinking in a new way of my father and his Brahmin ancestors, starving servants of the great temple" (*HL* 168). With the passage of each year in Africa Willie was acquiring new identities with new experiences. However, each time with a new experience he goes back to his ancestry and roots even though he has already denounced such a life of Indian ancestry with rules, codes and regulations. The postcolonial government in Africa was authoritarian though people thought that they were far away from the capital. The function of the postcolonial government was questionable in its approach to administration for giving people welfare governance because the authoritarian government heavily depended on some local people who exploited the resources of the country and practiced corrupt means for becoming richer and richer. Sometimes, the authoritarian government dumped the half-and-half man of Africa. Correia, a rich man of the colony, who transacted government business for commission was a Portuguese who had bank accounts abroad. But when there was a crisis in relation to the Govt. deal, such people were destroyed. Willie understood how a half man like him in a half-made African side could be destroyed any time. Naipaul's observations of this African life are rather convincingly illustrated here: "To destroy a Portuguese like himself would have been to break caste, according to the code of the colony, and to become disreputable. There was no trouble at all in throwing a man of the second rank into the darkness, someone from the half-and-half world, educated and respectable and striving unusually knowledgeable about money, and ready for many reasons to do whatever he might be required to do" (*HL* 174).

Willie's experiences along with Alvaro, the estate manager of the Correias in the warehouse were startling initially. It was a reflection of the great disorder in the African country in a postcolonial period when the army was pampered for the eventuality of an uprising or a war. The warehouse business was meant for the pleasures of the army soldiers. It was a shock for Willie to note that the tiny aged girls in the prime of their life are forced to such brutality of institutionalized prostitution for the pleasures of the soldiers and the other town people. It was an experience of horror, brutality and shock to Willie. He was surprised how the African waiters and the owners conducting the sex business could be so indifferent:

> I wish I had his detachment. But I was not trained for this kind of life, and I was full of shame.
>
> The girls were all African...but I wondered whether the two African waiters didn't suffer a little.
>
> And the girls were so young, so foolish, with so little idea ...of the way they were abusing their own bodies and darkening their lives I thought of my mother and I thought of my poor father who had hardly known what sex was. I thought of you too, Sarojini. I imagined that the girls might be you, and my heart shrunk. (*HL* 185)

Even Alvaro, who enjoyed the excitement of village sex every month with a fresh crop of innocent girls, was subdued in that warehouse. After that spur moment in that warehouse. Willie was disturbed a lot for his betrayal to Ana. However, there was a self-discovery in Willie in his experiences with the girl in that "split-second" when he was commanded by the tension of the body of the girl. However, it was a void, without any satisfaction, but this experience led him to a new idea of himself as a human being that he did not know during his life with Ana in the last ten years in Africa. That was so because both Ana and Willie were not guided by true sensuality or true desire. Willie had his own nervousness and fear at being in Africa. Even Ana had been half-timorous at that time of passion because of her family history. However, they led their half-life together: "We each found comfort in the other; and we had become very close, not looking beyond the other for satisfaction, not knowing, in fact, that another kind of satisfaction was possible" (*HL* 189). With such knowledge, Willie was moving in the wilderness for some years, but gradually that also became a mechanical experience with Willie in course of time. He therefore needed to revive with some new experience that was provided to him by Graca, Carla's convent-school friend, the wife of the new manager—at the German castle:

> The long drive had been a strain. Graca's need matched my own. That was new to me. Everything I had known before—the furtiveness of London, the awful Provincial prostitute, the paid black girls of the places of pleasure here, who had yet satisfied me for so long, and for whom for almost a year I had felt such gratitude, and poor Ana, still in my mind the trusting girl who had sat on the settee in my college room in London and allowed herself to be kissed, Ana still so gentle and generous—over the next half-hour everything fell away and I thought how terrible it would have been if, as could so easily have happened, I had died without knowing this depth of satisfaction, this other person that I had just discovered within myself. It was worth any price, any consequence. (*HL* 204-05)

The situations in postcolonial Africa were fluid, constantly changing the life of the common men in the colonies. The colonial government in the capital eased down and the Guerrillas took over. The Portuguese began to leave, and the army withdrew from the town. However, the army did not fight the African war in the town. The war was a distant game. It was rather tactical move to keep the town in peace. Graca's house, which she got through her friend Carla was taken for sharing. Her children were taken to Portugal. It was strange that the children were to prepare papers to say who they were. This was the problem of displacement and rootlessness. However, Ana was firm in not giving anything: "But I'm not running away. Half of what my grandfather gave me was stolen by my father. I will stay here and protect the other half. I do not want people squatting in my house or sleeping in my bed" (*HL* 226). After the normalcy, there was again rumor of a tribal war: "The guerrillas had had the support of the black Governments over the border. The new insurgents had the support of the white Government to the West, and they were far more deadly.... They raided the outskirts of towns and killed people and burnt houses and spread terror" (*HL* 226). Willie thought of leaving Africa because he would not be able to live through another war. Now that Willie was forty-one and had spent part of his life with Ana during the last eighteen years, he expressed his gratitude to her for obliging him. However, he had done nothing because he had led a half life by hiding there for a long time. To Willie, his life was a shadow life, the life of Ana rather than his own. Even to Ana, this was not her life either. The anguish of Willie is the result of shattering of all his illusions in the postcolonial scenario of Africa. After his dreams were shattered he prepared to go to Berlin, his sister, but then it was not his home. Willie had not yet arrived at his final identity. He was yet to explore something more about his identity. In this context, the anguish of Willie has been interpreted appropriately:

> Willie's anguish is not only his own but in a way, it also describes the agony of all individuals who have been separated by time and place. It is the anguish of people whose fondest dreams are ravaged and yet have something to fall back upon. (Mishra 136, *ACR* 3.2: 2004)

Half a Life therefore explores the predicament of an individual in postcolonial societies. The individual's high hopes and dreams of keeping away from his roots were frustrated finally, and the individual perhaps reconciles with his roots. His journey is spiritual because he acquires new experiences and through them a kind of new knowledge that evolves his identity. His identity is therefore not complete because experience does not end when he reaches Berlin. The novel ends there when Willie realizes the whole perspective of his journey from India to Africa via England. His identity is rather exploratory because it is continuously evolved, adding new experiences and new knowledge. Naipaul however takes up the crisis of Willie further when he returns to his sister, Sarojini in Berlin in his next novel *Magic Seeds*. In the next section, this will be discussed in greater detail.

Magic Seeds (2004)

Magic Seeds is a work of philosophical significance. It explores how life has its own ways and moves without being subjected to any structured pattern. This novel deals with the aftermath of African life of Willie who comes to Berlin to his sister, Sarojini, after spending a "half-life" with his wife Ana. Perhaps Willie Chandran tries to explore his identity soon after coming back to his sister, but his sister does not approve of

Willie's actions because she believes he has run away from life by escaping to face the guerrilla war. Such cowardly action is denounced by her completely. She therefore persuades him to join the guerrilla war perpetuated by the Tamils in the Indian forests, where he later on spends seven years among the revolutionaries. Then he is also imprisoned. After the release, he goes to London once again after a gap of thirty years. He however experiences London to be quite different in the late 1980s/early 1990s. It is important to note the evolutionary significance of Willie as an individual. Through the journeys of his life, he goes to London from India, then moves to Africa, from Africa to Berlin, then to the Indian forests and jail, and therefrom to London. His homelessness sometimes makes him a romantic to have a house of his own like Mr. Biswas in the epic novel of Naipaul, *A House for Mr. Biswas.* It is quite interesting to note his psychological set-up and mature reactions to this world which is not governed by any design by an individual:

> All night Willie heard the music. It invaded his sleep and mingled with other memories. Africa, with the conical grey stone hills and Africans walking on the red paths beside the asphalt road. The burnt-out concrete houses, smoke-stained around the windows. The forest and the men in olive uniform with caps with the red stain star, and the endless marching. The strange jail where, as on a slave ship, the prisoners lay side by side on the floor in two rows separated by a central aisle. All night it seemed to him as well that he had found something good to write to Sarojini about. This thing eluded him. He looked for it, through all the slave music, and in the morning all he was left with was, "It is wrong to have an ideal view of the world. That's where the mischief starts. That's where everything starts unraveling. But I can't write to Sarojini about that." (*MAS* 280)

The novel ends with such a state of mind of Willie, the protagonist. Willie has attempted to write a letter, but fails because he changes his mind three or four times every week. As a result he writes the letters, but neither completes them nor sends any one of them to his sister.

Going back to Willie's life often years back, it is quite interesting to understand his frame of mind. When he divorces his wife Ana after living with her for eighteen years, he thinks that he may lead a full life in future if he leaves Africa. But, in Berlin his sister challenges his "running away" and "hiding" life without facing the hard realities. Sarojini straightaway reminds him of his short existence in Berlin because his visa cannot be renewed:

> Another World. He was living there in a temporary, half-and-half way with his sister Sarojini. After Africa it had been a great refreshment, this new kind of protected life, being almost a tourist, without demands, without anxiety. It had to end, of course; it had begun to end the day Sarojini said to him. 'You've been here for six months. I may not be able to get your visa renewed again. You know what that means. You may not be able to stay here. That's the way the world is made. You can't object to it. You've got to start thinking of moving on. Do you have any idea of where you can go?' (*MAS* 5)

As usual, life is not subject to well-structured design to Willie. He therefore says: "I don't see what I can do. I don't know where I can go" (*MAS* 5). When Sarojini reprimands him for his callous attitude in life he questions: "What could I have done in India? What could I have done in England in 1957 or 1958? Or in Africa?" (*MAS* 6). But Sarojini is aggressive towards her brother: "You've always preferred to hide. It's the colonial psychosis, the caste psychosis. You inherited it from your father. You were in Africa for eighteen years. There was a great guerrilla war there. Didn't you know?" (*MAS* 6).

She further elaborates the significance of the guerrilla war:

> It was a glorious war. At least in the beginning when you think about it, it can bring tears to the eyes. A poor and helpless people, slaves in their own land, starting from scratch in every way.
>
> What did you do? Did you seek them out? Did you join them? Did you help them? That was a big enough cause to any one looking for a cause. But no. You stayed in your

> estate house with your lovely little half-white wife and pulled the pillow over your ears and hoped that no bad black freedom fighter was going to come in the night with a gun and heavy boots and frighten you. (*MAS* 6)

She suggested her brother that he should have joined the war the African revolution, for the cause of liberating the people of Africa. When Sarojini was reprimanding him, a Tamil rose-seller, a revolutionary is seen selling roses. Citing the activities of this Tamil revolutionary who is working for the cause of liberation of the Tamils, Sarojini tells his brother that the rose-seller has more worth than Willie because he has found his war. He is brave enough to face the reality whereas Willie has not that courage. Sarojini argues that it is necessary to know the authenticity of history to understand a revolution in its proper perspective: "He had the look of a man with a cause, the look of a man apart. It's something you might have noticed in Africa, if you had learned to look. This man's selling roses here, but those roses are being turned to guns. Somewhere else far away. It's how revolutions are made. There is no more disciplined guerrilla army in the world. They are quite ferocious, quite ugly. And if you know more about your own history you would understand what a miracle that is" (*MAS* 9-10).

Sarojini's interpretation of history of India from the point of view of imperialism is quite significant. She believes that the first history book about India written by a British school Inspector is biased and, not authentic representation of facts because Roper Lethbridge, the historian has been motivated by the imperialistic bias. Even then, his British way of presenting facts, though commercial, still gave us some learning:

> One of the most important of those ideas was that in India there were servile races, people born to be slaves and there were martial races. The martial races were fine; the senile races were not. You and I half belong to the servile races. I am sure you know that. I am sure you half accept that. That is why you have lived as you have lived. The Tamils selling roses in Berlin belong wholly to the servile races. That idea would have even been impressed on them in all

> kinds of ways. And that British idea about the servile and the martial races of India is utterly wrong. (*MAS* 10)

Such deconstruction of history deserves special mention because it leads us to rethink how the British administration is denigrating the Indian people in their own land. That is the functioning of imperialism: "It is what happens to captive people" (*MAS* 11). Sarojini further explains: "Since in India we have no idea of history we quickly forget our past and always believe what we are told" (*MAS* 11).

In the new British dispensation, the Tamils in the South were considered dirt, fit only for labor for which they were sent off as serfs to the plantations of Malay and Ceylon and other places. Sarojini pleads before Willie that these Tamils who are selling roses to buy guns are the truly martial races who have thrown off a great weight of history and propaganda: "They have made themselves a truly martial people and they have done so against the odds. You must respect them, Willie" (*MAS* 11).

Sarojini's assertive talk on injustice and cruelty, and the need for revolution has the force of serenity to have a great influence on Willie. Sarojini's understanding of the politics of revolution has equipped her with a complete intellectual system: "Her worldview was able to absorb everything: political murders in Guatemala, Islamic revolution in Iran, caste riots in India and even the petty theft practiced as a matter of shop keeping habit or principle by the wine-shop men in Berlin..." (*MAS* 12). Willie now sees a Sarojini of a different kind. She has evolved to understand everything with so much calmness and poise. By staying with his sister for six months in Berlin, "the world began to change for him. Just as he felt she could enter all his emotions...so he began to enter her way of looking. There was a logic and order in everything he said" (*MAS* 13). Sarojini has shown Willie the two worlds: one is ordered and settled where people live quite happy; and the other world is desperate to enter the simpler, ordered world. In this sound world, "a hundred loyalties, the residue of old history tied them down; a hundred little wars filled them with hate and dissipated their energies" (*MAS* 13). In Berlin, Willie understood that the two worlds co-existed. Going back to his life twenty years back, he felt ashamed: "His half life in London: and then all his life in Africa, that life when he was permanently in semi-hiding, gauging his success by the fact that in his second class, semi-Portuguese group he didn't particularly stand out, and was "passing": all that life seemed shameful" (*MAS* 14). He therefore decided that he would no more lead a life of hiding and would join some revolution.

Sarojini referring to history one day, while both of them were walking below the trees in the shopping avenue, told Willie that Kandapalli would be comparable to Lenin or Mao when the history of the twentieth century revolution would be written in future. He is an important person because he has the capacity to bend the course of history: "When, in a hundred years, the definitive history of twentieth century revolution comes to be written, and various ethnocentric prejudices have disappeared Kandapalli will be up there with Lenin and Mao of that I have no doubt. And you haven't even heard of him now" (*MAS* 15). To Kandapalli, "Revolution was to come, from below from the village, from the people. There was to be no place in this movement for middle class masqueraders" (*MAS* 18). Kandapalli has been able to spearhead a true revolution. He is a simple man from Warangal, a school teacher without qualifications, is always moved with tears, when he talks about the poor, the marginalized sections of the society.

During his five months stay in Berlin with his sister, Willie was given the mental exercise of thinking about the desperate places of the world he had known: "He found himself reconsidering Africa and his marriage, acknowledging everything in a new way, hiding nothing, submerging all the pathos of his non-descript past in an ennobling new ideal" (*MAS* 14). The knowledge of his own "self" and other things and situations as well brought a new kind of joy in Willie: "at the same time he felt the excitement of the new movements of his heart and mind: and he felt above everything around him" (*MAS* 25). Willie's condition of homelessness as a refugee from Africa with no place to go to had not dumped him like many others who were to lead a life of a tramp like another Indian he met in Berlin, who was having "no place to sleep, his mind no longer whole, his breath very bad, a broken arm in a sling black with grime, complaining of his torments at the hands of young thugs" (*MAS* 25). He understood that he had spent a shameless life in Africa, but his varied experiences and false longings of the past were only a preparation for what was to come to him in the near future. After a letter from Joseph to her husband Wood, Sarojini would tell her brother that he would meet that university teacher in India to join the revolution of Kandapalli which was being regulated by him in his forest headquarters. It was therefore a great chance for Willie to go to India after a gap of twenty years: "After more than twenty years Willie saw India again. He had left India with very little money, the gift of his father; and he was going back with very little money, the gift of his sister" (*MAS* 28).

Willie in India understands now that he has a different identity. Twenty years ago he had gone to England with the identity of his father's son to study for a degree/diploma in England. In the meanwhile, through different phases of his life in London, Africa and Berlin he has become a different man. He therefore sees India from a different perspective when he reaches in the airport:

> Twenty years ago I wouldn't have seen what I am seeing now. I am seeing what I see because I have made myself another person. I cannot make myself that old person again. But I must go back to that old way of seeing. Otherwise my cause is lost before I have begun. I have come from a world of waste and appearances. I saw quite clearly some time ago that it was a simple world, where people had been simplified. I must not go back on that vision. I must understand that now I am among people of more complicated beliefs and social ideas, and at the same time in a world stripped of all style and artifice. This is an airport. It works. It is full of technically accomplished people. That is what I must see. (*MAS* 30)

From the airport Willie went to the distant town of Joseph by a train. When they had their initiation to each other Joseph told Willie about his impressions of Africa:

> Like you, my attitude to Africa was the colonial one. But that's where we all have to begin. It was the colonialists who opened up Africa and told us about it.... We are in

> one of the saddest places in the world here. Twenty times sadder than what you saw in Africa. In Africa the colonial past would have been there for you to see. Here you can't begin to understand the past, and when you get to know it you wish you didn't. (*MAS* 38-39)

Joseph goes back to the Indian history of four hundred years back to illustrate the catastrophe that fell on this sacred last Indian kingdom which was invaded by the Muslims to destroy the kingdom completely.

After ruining the capital city, they killed the entire human resources and talent: "they killed the priests the philosophers, the artisans, the architects, the scholars" (*MAS* 39). The only people spared were the serfs, the low class people during this military defeat. It was a "war of annihilation, a war without limits and restraints" (*MAS* 40). There was no resistance against this destructive war. The serfs were the people who were completely divided. "They were of various low castes, and there is no caste hatred greater than that of the low, one up-caste for another" (*MAS* 39). They all belonged to serving class, slaves in some sense. After the great demolition and destruction they ruled people by force and imposed forty types of taxes. As a result, people were to live with much poverty. Through such rules of exploitation people have now thought that this is their eternal condition of poverty and slavery. Joseph further interprets how the people did not have a sense of dignity and rage against such destructions and exploitations. They are rather callous and indifferent to their self-dignity:

> But this was the origin of our sacred Indian poverty, the poverty that India could offer the world. And there was something else. Thirty years after the destruction of the last Indian Kingdom the conquerors built a big gate of victory. The gate of victory is now an Indian heritage site. The destroyed city has been forgotten. (*MAS* 40)

Joseph has been enraged to its climax when he utters that there should have been a great revenge by the rulers after independence. But that did not happen:

> Defeat can be terrible. You would have thought that at independence all the lords of the conquered people would

> have been hanged with their families and their bodies left to turn to bones. That would have been a kind of redemption, the beginning of something new. But nothing like that happened. It was left to some very simple people to raise the standard of revolution. (*MAS* 40-41)

The extremist revolutionary outrage of Joseph is quite conspicuous in his anger of expression: "Yes. I would leave nothing better than to see a revolution sweeping everything away" (*MAS* 42). He also suggested Willie to move to Neo Anand Bhavan from the hotel Riviera because none of the revolutionaries would come to see him in such a high class hotel. In Neo Anand Bhavan, Willie would have the "tormenting" and "emptiest" days? With the new way of life he has come to terms. Willie is a bit disturbed: "I have to understand now that, in this venture, books are a cheat. I have to depend on my own resources" (*MAS* 46). Being now trapped, he reflects: "I no longer know where I am. I don't think I will be able to pick up my way back. I am in their hands now" (*MAS* 48). Willie's state of mind is derailing in the early days of the forest life. That is why he questioned himself why he jumped into the revolution of Kandapalli:

> Kandapalli wished the villagers and the poor to fight their own battles. I am not among the poor and villagers in this camp. There has been some mistake. I have fallen among the wrong people. I have come to the wrong revolution. I don't like these faces. And yet I have to be with them. I have to get a message out to Sarojini or to Joseph. But I don't know how. (*MAS* 50)

Willie's predicament in the forest is well understood because he has gone there to join the revolution after his life of high luxury in Africa and Berlin. One night when he is asked to do sentry duty, Willie becomes emotional and cries: "That night Willie cried, tears of rage, tears of fear, and in the dawn the cry of the peacock, after it had drunk from its forest pool, filled him with grief for the whole world" (*MAS* 50). In the training camp of the organization, Willie was not feeling comfortable. He was however to hide his feelings. He could not be explicit to make his disgust known to these people: "I have never known such boredom. Ever since I have come to India I have known these terrible nights of boredom. I suppose it is a kind of training, a kind of asceticism, but for what I am not sure. I must look upon it as another chamber of experience. I must give no sign to these people that I am no: absolutely with them" (*MAS* 52). Willie could not comprehend the causes of the trainee mates, who were all in their mid-lives, to join such a revolution. During the camp life, Willie thought of going to the poor people to understand their "unreserved sorrows over the centuries". From the training camp, Willie was sent to the village Dulhipur along with Bhoj Narayan who guided him in all critical situations.

With the meagre amount of ₹ 150, both of them were to ration money for daily expenses to survive in the forest. Willie's patience was now lost without money. He thought of running away, but Bhoj Narayan guided him to keep patience, and if possible they might return to the forest wherefrom they came. Keeping his conscience he did not run away: "It is cowardly. It is against all my knowledge of the world. I must never think of it again" (*MAS* 76). The idea of home is very much important for Willie. Willie looks for home everywhere. Even in the bagasse yard he looked at home. He is always disturbed by the idea of home: "It's the one thing I have worked at all my life: not being at home anywhere, but looking at home" (*MAS* 74). Being on the move always. Willie along with Bhoj Narayan enjoyed the duty of a courier. To him as a courier, the guerrilla territory was no more a series of unconnected landscapes: "This being on the move pleased him, gave him a feeling of purpose and drama, though he could only intuit the general guerrilla situation. Part of his business as a man who traveled was to give encouragement, to exaggerate the extent of the liberated areas, to suggest that in many areas the war was almost on the point of being won, and required only one last push" (*MAS* 75). Bhoj Narayan, the revolutionary and companion to Willie suspected Raja, the weaver, whose last deliveries of supplies were captured by the police. Thinking that both Raja and his elder brother would be a great threat by passing information to police, Bhoj shot Raja dead. Near the post office, when Bhoj Narayan was captured by the police, Willie was on his own way to a village by a passenger train. However, he became too much reflective on the two lives

—Bhoj's and Raja's—which were wasted after the success stories of their family lineage of two or three generations. There were possibilities of prosperity. But these two lives came to nothing.

At this juncture of his life Willie was in crisis because he had been trapped in such a revolutionary organization from which he could not escape. Sometimes a sort of emptiness and frustration had shaken him. Therefore he was thinking of death as an escape from this state of psychological crisis: "The most comforting thing about life is the certainty of death. There is no way now for me to pick my way back to the upper air. Where was the upper air? Berlin? Africa?" (*MAS* 103). Willie's role in the revolutionary organization was suddenly changed from a courier to a member under the commander Ramachandra, a bony handsome man with a gun, AK 47. Under the chairmanship of the leader, the section meeting took place in the hut of Ramachandra for about three hours. Many issues were discussed including the loss of the squad which was inevitable in any kind of revolution or war. The leader further argued that it was not a ripe time to expand the revolutionary base in the small towns. It was rather important to expand the bases in the villages in the deep forest areas. Einstein, a critic of Kandapalli, pleaded for a shift in change to the approach of the revolution because the peasants, from which background he himself came, were to be roughed up a bit to be disciplined in the organization. Even he pleaded that people like Shivdas needed the help of the revolutionaries to enhance his wealth: "But (Shivdas) is a crook and a thug. The big landowners and the old feudal officials have run away. There is no policeman or surveyor in his village, and every year Shivdas reaps many acres of the other people's crops and ploughs many acres of other people's land. If people didn't think we were with him, they would have killed him long ago. The day Shivdas thinks it will serve him better he will betray us to the police" (*MAS* 104). Such type of neo-colonial situation exists in many villages. A revolutionary, according to Einstein should have clarity of vision and precision of thought. He therefore now blames Willie for the misfortune befell on their commander Bhoj Narayan because of such lack of vision and clear thoughts. Though generously Willie accepted his mistake, he was highly appreciated by the leader. Finally, it was resolved that the revolutionary base should be expanded in the deep forest among the villages.

This new idea of liberating more areas in the villages of forest was a strange thing for Willie: "It was a step down into yet another kind of life; patternless labour without reward or goal, without solitude or companionship; without news of the outside world, with no prospect of letters from Sarojini, with nothing to anchor himself to" (*MAS* 105-06). In the deep forest, Willie developed some sort of relationship for which he gave an outline of his experience in England, Africa and Berlin. Ramachandra explains that his idea of revolution is different from Kandapalli. As a revolutionary, Kandapalli believes in dialogue whereas Ramachandra and many others believe that revolution can be achieved through blood and violence. The young people who join the revolution believe in action and change. However the villagers, who are landless and poor, are not accepting the suggestion to take over the land. To them the land does not belong to them, so they cannot plough. To bring them to sense, you need violence so that there will be radical changes in the society and the landless poor will be free from their slavery mentality. Having faith in revolution, they will think that their poverty is not permanent and the idea that the poor will remain poor and the rich will remain rich will go away. Ramachandra's idea of revolution to transform the villages through social equality has a flaw. Willie therefore thinks: "They all want the old ways to go. But the old ways are part of people's being. If the old ways go, people will not know who they are, and these villages, which have their own beauty, will become a jungle" (*MAS* 117). The background of Ramachandra being a revolutionary lies in his poverty and shame. "Shame" is eternal. It can only die with the person who has been ashamed: "Little things drive people more than we sometimes imagine. I have so many causes of shame. In India, London and Africa. They are fresh after twenty tears. I don't think they will ever die. They will die only with me" (*MAS* 120). Ramachandra, the commander with a gun, has to grow his strength and skill to face the police. He was therefore killed in the police encounter and after which Willie and others were to go back on their tracks for their survival. Willie is now puzzled what to do: "Now I'm truly lost. In every way. I don't know what lies ahead or behind. My only cause now is to survive, to get out of this" (*MAS* 122).

So Willie and others came back to their old places after the wish of the high command to extend the liberated areas had failed. Different section meetings were conducted to chalk out the plan for further action when police arrested their leader of the forest and also Kandapalli, the leader with humanity and tears for the poor. However, all their plans failed even to kidnap a minister to protest the arrest of Kandapalli. It was therefore presumed that the movement could not be run any further. There was more brutal action by the police. Finally, Einstein and Willie also decided to surrender to the police in a planned manner. That was done with meticulous care and caution. Willie had the idea that soon after his surrender, he might be arrested and released afterwards. But his case was seriously viewed because of the killing of three policemen by Ramachandra and he was close to him. Though he himself was idle and not involved in any murder during his revolutionary days, he was charged as an accessory which was quite unfair. After his worried London life and African life of purposelessness and Berlin plan Willie's revolutionary life was rather a life of a floater: "But he had been undone by the India of his return. He could see no pattern, no thread. He had returned with an idea of action, of truly placing himself in the world. But he had become a floater, and the world had become more phantasmagoric than it had ever been. That unsettling feeling, of phantasmagoria had come to him the day when poor Raja, with boyish excitement, had taken him for a ride in his three-wheel scooter, to show him the "enemy" (*MAS* 150-51). Willie, after the hearing in the court, was sentenced to ten years' imprisonment. However after some days, his sister came to visit him in his jail and therefore planned his release. As a result of which Willie, released from the prison under terms of special amnesty, went to London: "Willie understood that just as his father, thirty years ago, had by his begging letters to great men in England set certain wheels in motion that had eventually taken him to London, so now Sarojini, out of her great political experience, had begun to act on his behalf" (*MAS* 168).

At every stage of his life, Willie is disturbed by the question of his identity. So in London, he felt his old stirrings and the beginning of old grief. He then made up his mind: "I have been there. I have given part of my life and I have nothing to show for it. I cannot go there again. I must let that part of me die. I must lose that vanity. I must understand that big countries grow or shrink according to the play of international forces that are beyond the control of any one man. I must try now to be only myself, if such a tuning is possible" (*MAS* 169-70). Reflecting upon his adaptation of his delicate brain to all these changing situations including his tormented life in the jail he tells Roger: "The whole thing was so strange, such a string of unreal episodes, I feel in time I would have gone mad like the others. The brain is so delicate, and man can adapt to so many situations. That's how it's been for me" (*MAS* 172). Roger tells him that in some ways life has been the same for everybody. However, unlike Willie, Roger has always lived in the real world. Contrarily Willie's life has been full of surprises without having any control over things. That night Willie had a heavy sleep in Roger's house after taking a large amount of whisky. Awakening, he was disturbed a lot when he thought of his homelessness: "I have never slept in a room of my own. Never at home in India, when I was a boy. Never here in London. Never in Africa. I lived in somebody else's house always, and slept in somebody else's bed. In the forest of course there were no rooms, and then the jail was the jail. Will I ever sleep in a room of my own?" (*MAS* 177-78). Such a thought had never occurred to him. This idea of homelessness is an important diasporic consciousness. Even Naipaul himself has often been disturbed by such an idea though willingly he led such a life of homelessness. Perdita met him in the room and showed him his paperback ball and also told him how Roger made the plan of his release from the jail through this book arguing that he is not a political writer, but a real one. Willie read that "his book was a pioneer of Indian postcolonial writing" (*MAS* 180). Walking in the streets of London, Willie thought that he was a free man. He was not bound by any organization to join for a revolution as when he came to India from Berlin. He is now a completely free man: "Now I can only celebrate what I am or what I have become" (*MAS* 188). After two weeks Willie's mood of exaltation vanished because of the repetitive, mechanical life he had fallen into. Since he had already seen enough of London life, he therefore did not get any pleasure. Even his past life in London was not exciting. Willie wanted to join a job because he was feeling bored day-by-day. Roger suggested that work might make him a slave. A man might get some self-fulfillment in work, but then seeing people at work in the office made him awful. Willie however got a job in the magazine office at Bloomsbury, London for which he was to go in the morning. After six weeks in the Bloomsbury office Willie went to Barnet, to be trained in architecture in the company's training centre. When Roger drove Willie to the training centre, Willie saw on the way the immigrant Indians, Pakistanis and Bangladeshis from the subcontinent that repeopled London during the last thirty years assuming that London is still the centre, not a periphery. When Roger dropped Willie in the hostel, he talked about his crises and problems in personal life. Willie however found the course at the training centre richer and profounder sidelining the problems of his friend in his mind. The course on architecture interested Willie significantly because whatever he learnt was quite relevant to correlate to what he saw around him. However, at this late age he began to learn things and saw life in a new way:

> It is terrible and heartbreaking that this way of seeing and understanding has come to me so late. I can't do anything with it now. A man of fifty cannot remake his life. I have heard it said that the only difference between the rich and the poor in a certain kind of economy is that the rich have money ten or fifteen or twenty years before the poor. (*MAS* 220)

In the same manner people who come to see things in a way quite late, they are fools. He therefore mocks at all those attending the courses because all of them are in the forties or fifties who have already crossed the prime of their life. People from various countries as South Africa, Australia, Egypt, India, Pakistan, Malaysia, China and so on were sent by their companies to undergo the training in this course, "to get at knowledge that was simply there seemingly divinely provided, knowledge that had for a long time been unfairly denied them for racial or political reasons but was now, in a miraculously changed world, theirs to claim as their own. And this claimed knowledge confirmed each man in the Tightness of his own racial or tribal or religious ways" (*MAS* 225).

Though Willie enjoyed the course, in the weekends he felt desolated and nostalgic when other trainees moved to different places. He went back to his roots, his past life in Africa and India. He became emotional when he thought of the misfortunes of his "caste" father and "low caste" mother: "understanding as a result with the deepest kind of ache that there was no true place in the world for him-back to that childhood when on some especially unhappy evenings there came, with the utmost clarity, a child's vision of the earth spinning in darkness, with everyone on it lost" (*MAS* 228).

Willie was not alone undergoing tremendous psychological pressure by being uprooted from his roots. Even Roger in his own country had his own predicament. As a friend of Willie, Roger opened his heart to him and when he talked about his crisis, both personal and that of country tears rolled down his cheeks: "He talked of socialism and high taxes, and the inflation that inevitably followed high taxes, destroxing families and the idea of families. This idea of families (rather than the family) passed on values from one generation to the next. These shared values held a country together; the loss of these values broke a country up, hastened a general decline" (*MAS* 233). Roger, like Willie himself, believed in liberal ideas. He was a man of "inherited liberal ideas, a man rooted in this liberalism, concerned with human rights all over the world, and at the same time at ease with his country's recent history going with flow" (*MAS* 233). However, Roger had his own personal tragedy with Marian though she had long back inspired him to work with optimism. Willie now writes a letter of optimism to his sister, Sarojini regarding his plan for future. He would study architecture for next eight years; then he would work about fifteen years till seventy-five. By that way, he could at least lead an active and satisfying life of ten to fifteen years in the profession: "The difficulty there is that to any logical mind it is absurd for a man of fifty to start learning a profession. The main difficulty is that to carry it out I would need an injection of optimism" (*MAS* 271). He further writes to his sister: If I was born now, in the same place, the world would have a different look. Too late for me unfortunately. And with that pathetic little self that now exists inside me somewhere, the self that I recognize so easily, I put aside the architecture dream and think that I should get some understanding little job somewhere and live in some little flat somewhere and hope that the neighbours are not too noisy. But I know enough now to understand that life can never be simplified like that and that there would be some little trap or flow in that dream of simplicity, of just letting one's life pass, of treating one's life only as a way of passing the time (*MAS* 272). That is how most of the dreams in life remain unfulfilled. These dreams are the "magic seeds" which never fertilize, never grow. However, these "seeds" remain optimism in life to move on. Willie writes to his sister that a successful man is a happy man who has "precise goals, limited and attainable" (*MAS* 272) like his friend Marcus whose only goal was to have sex with white women and have a white grandchild. He has succeeded in achieving both: "His half-English son, Lyndhurst, now a man of about thirty, has had two children by a pure-white aristocratic lady. One of these children is as white as white can be. The whole thing is being sealed this Saturday by the wedding of the half-English boy and his lady, mother of his white child. It is the fashion here, babies before wedding bells" (*MAS* 272-73). Referring to the wedding of Marcus's son and his son's two children before marriage, Naipaul perhaps suggests that these two children—white and black—are the magic seeds who would grow in future. He has brought out the racial memory and the slave music in the wedding. Further the dreams of the individuals, which are not precise, may be thought of as the magic seeds, which are not often easily achievable. They seem to be things in a magic, in a dream. However, the "magic seeds"—the optimism in life—may make life move on to an unknown future. This is the blurred identity of an individual who is moving towards "the unknown" submerged in the dreams to achieve the magic seeds in his life.

IV

Naipaul thinks that the "idea of flux" is always positive because it refreshes civilization and moves it forward in the path of some significant progress. In Naipaul's later novels including the last two interpreted in this paper, there is an integration of myth, history, autobiography and fiction to emphasize the relevance of an "awareness of history" of the individual and the whole community to understand the present in the right perspective. Naipaul believes that every individual only knows a part of his identity because he does not know much about his ancestry and origin beyond his grandfather. Analyzing the anarchy and cruelty of colonialism he brings "the sufferings of the margins during colonialism" into focus. In the context of the diasporic identity of the displaced, he emphasizes that these rootless people without a history, do not even develop an awareness of history to understand their predicament of displacement. Naipaul understands that there is no set pattern in which the world is to be governed. The different ways of governance should be understood in the context of history, politics, and culture of a place, individual and community. It is therefore significant to note that identity is not merely an issue to be related to either inheritance or history, but it is to be governed by both. The core issue of identity is related to homelessness, displacement and multiple associations of diasporic aspects. Naipaul's *Half a Life,* as we have already seen, is about a search for identity of the protagonist Willie Chandran. His search remains incomplete even at the end of the novel. In India and England, Willie has no identity of his own. Even in Africa he has no distinctive identity because he has only lived a half-life. His life is unreal and meaningless with his wife Ana in her native land Africa. The search for an existential life for Willie remains unfulfilled because his life is "half-discovered, half-realized and half-lived" (Choubey 2002: 1). We have already interpreted how the novel is about half-lives of various people: the various predicaments of various half-made societies and peoples. Whenever there is a war or uprising, change in government or racial/ethnic conflicts, the greatest sufferers are the people who have always been under threat. Willie, being a migrant in London and Africa and a postcolonial writer, has a deeper understanding of the cultural life of London and Africa than the natives of England and Africa respectively. Willie's existential suffering as an exile in the multiracial society of Portuguese Africa affected him so much that he developed an attitude to assert his identity. The crisis of identity has also been with his father who has been displaced from roots in his own society. When he has established his identity as a spiritual man, he is later on disappointed to observe that his son Willie is drifting away from him. So when Willie goes to London, he has tried to reconstruct his identity as a postcolonial writer. However, after writing his only book, he has again been displaced from his identity when he accompanies Ana, his wife, to her native land Africa, where he would live only a half-life. He therefore goes to Berlin, where his sister Sarojini is living. During his stay in Africa, a strange country with a strange language, Willie has acquired new-identities with new experience by the passage of each year. However, with new experiences each time he goes back to his ancestry in search of his roots despite the fact that he has denounced the rigidity of his ancestral life in India with its own codes and regulations. Willie has been shocked when he experiences the harshness and authoritarianism of the postcolonial government in Africa towards the "half-and-half" men of Africa. We have already discussed the chaos and disorder in the postcolonial society in Africa without a concrete vision for moving forward. There is no stability in the life of common men. They have been subjected to the whims of the visionless government and recklessness of the rebels. In such a situation, Willie's dreams and illusions have been shattered because of the postcolonial scenario in Africa. His anguish is that he has no role to play as he has no identity of his own. He therefore moves on, being displaced once again, in search of his final identity. But even after reaching Berlin, he cannot attain it. The novel ends with the predicament of Willie in a postcolonial society. However his spiritual journey that has started with his departure from India to reach Africa via England has not yet been complete because his new experiences and new kinds of knowledge help in his evolution of an identity which is not final. In an attempt to reconcile with his roots, Willie once again tries to amend his way of life, and decides to go to India to join a revolution by which his identity has again been displaced. This aspect of his life has been taken up by Naipaul in *Magic Seeds,* Naipaul's last novel so far.

This novel has also dealt with Willie's exploration of further identity after the failure of African experience. Willie joins the guerrilla revolution in the Indian forests for seven years, and thereafter he is imprisoned. His dreams of revolutionising the society fail. His magic seeds do not grow. They are never fertilized. Life is not moving on a set pattern. It is not as simple as that. Even then for living on, one needs "magic seeds" in life because they inspire him to live on, to be optimistic to attain the unachievable to strive for the unreal. A man with "magic seeds" as his dreams may often be unsuccessful like Willie because a successful man is a happy man who has "precise goals, limited and attainable" (*MAS* 272). But Willie's goal is not limited for which he cannot move according to some set patterns that can be achieved easily. It is therefore imperative on the part of Willie to strive for a "blurred identity" by moving towards the unknown submerged in the dreams to achieve the magic seeds in his life, to attain the unrealized abstraction rather than a concrete future. In contrast to the life of Willie, his friend Marcus has a set goal to have white grandchildren which he achieves easily. If these two grandchildren of Marcus—one white and the other black—are to be regarded as magic seeds, they would rather enliven the "racial memory" and "slave music" that may also be quite disturbing in future life. Willie as an individual in *Magic Seeds* is evolutionary. A life without a set pattern as Willie has, moves in a cyclic process—from India to England, from England to Africa, from Africa to Berlin, from Berlin to India, and then from India to England again. In his movements "place" is significant undoubtedly. However, the individual is constant-displaced, and his acquired identities are continuously changed in time and space. It is just like magic because Willie's dreams are never fulfilled. That is why Willie now understands in his second stint in London that "it is wrong to have an ideal view of the world. That is where the mischief starts. That is where everything starts unraveling" (*MAS* 280). This is a great realization for Willie after so many experiences in his life. It is the greatest treasure of his wisdom. Self-realization is the highest wisdom an individual acquires in his life. Naipaul's emphasis on a "sense of history" is also found in Sarojini's interpretation of history of India where she deconstructs the history written by the British historian who is a school inspector. Sarojini argues that such representation of history is rather based on "suppressed" facts. It has no authenticity, and hence untrue. History should be based on truth, the facts of life. Sarojini is unhappy that people in India do not bother for their past because they lack the "historical sense". However Sarojini further asserts that the Tamils are a truly martial race who is fighting against injustice. Even the Tamils who are selling rose flowers to support their guerrilla war in the Indian jungles are against the cruelty and injustice done to the marginalized, the deprived class. Sarojini's revolutionary thinking and understanding of the poetics of revolution have the force of serenity to have a great impact on Willie to join the guerrilla revolution in his ancestral land to realise his "dreams of change" in the society, to grow the magic seeds to their maturity. In the process, he has now acquired new experiences that spiritualize his thinking.

Works Consulted and Cited

Barua, Krishna. "'I Must not Unpack': The Rhetorics of Hiding in V.S. Naipaul's *Half a Life*." *The Atlantic Critical Review*, 3.2 (2004): 116-28.

Bhat, Yashoda. *V.S. Naipaul: An Introduction*. New Delhi: BR Publication, 2000.

Boehmer, Elleke. *Colonial and Postcolonial Literature*. New Delhi: UP, 2008.

Choubey, Asha. "A Critique of Naipaul's *Half a Life:* Searching for Identity in Limbo", http//65.107.211.208/Caribbean/naipaul/Choubey3.html. 2002.

Engdahl, Dr. Horace. "On Naipaul" in *V.S. Naipaul: Critical Essays*. Vol. III. Mohit K. Ray, ed. New Delhi: Atlantic, 2005.

———. "The Presentation Speech" in *V.S. Naipaul: Critical Essays*. Vol. III, Mohit K. Ray, ed. New Delhi: Atlantic, 2005.

French, Patrick. *The World is what it is: The Authorized Biography of V.S. Naipaul.* London: Picador, 2008.

Greenblatt, S.J. *Learning to Curse: Essays in Modern Literature.* New York: Routledge, 1990.

Haldar, Santwana. "V.S. Naipaul's *Half a Life:* The Colonial Context and Some Post Colonial issues" in *V.S. Naipaul: Critical Essays,* Vol. III. Mohit K. Ray, ed. New Delhi: Atlantic Publishers, 2005: 226-49.

Jones, Stephanie. *The Journal of Commonwealth Literature.* Vol. 35, No. 1, 2000.

Joshi, Chandra B. *V.S. Naipaul: The Voice of Exile.* New Delhi: Sterling Publishers, 1984.

Kamra, Shashi. *The Novels of V.S. Naipaul.* New Delhi: Prestige, 1990.

King, Bruce. *V.S. Naipaul.* Houndmills, Basingstoke, Hampshire and London: Macmillan, 1993.

Mishra, Binod. "Return and Reconciliation in V.S. Naipaul's *Half a Life*" in *The Atlantic Critical Review.* 3.2 (2004): 129-38.

Mishra, Pankaj, Ed. "Introduction" in *Literary Occasions: V.S. Naipaul.* Oxford: Picador, 2004.

Mustafa, Fawzia. *V.S. Naipaul: An Introduction.* New Delhi: BR Publication, 2000.

Naipaul, Seepersad. *The Adventures of Gurudeva.* New Delhi: Buffalo Books, 2001 (India edition).

Naipaul. V.S. *Guerrillas.* London: Picador, 2002.

———. *A Bend in the River.* London: Picador, 2002.

———. *The Enigma of Arrival.* London: Picador, 2002.

———. *A Way in the World.* London: Vintage, 2001.

———. *Half a Life.* London: Picador, 2002.

———. *Magic Seeds.* New York: Vintage, 2005.

———. "Conrad's Darkness and Mine" in *Literary Occasions.* Oxford: Picador, 2004: 162-80.

———. "Prologue to an Autobiography" in *Literary Occasions.* Oxford: Picador, 2004: 53-111.

———. *A Writers People.* London: Picador, 2008.

———. *Literary-Occasions: Essays.* London: Picador, 2004.

———. *The Writer and the World: Essays.* London: Picador, 2003.

———. *Finding the Centre.* London: Penguin, 1985.

———. *Reading and Writing: A Personal Account.* New York: New York Review of Books, 2000.

Nandan, S. "The Diasporic Consciousness" in *Interrogating Post Colonialism: Theory, Text and Context.*

Panwar, P. ed. *V.S. Naipaul: An Anthology of Recent Criticism.* Delhi: Pencraft International, 2007.

Pradhan, Prakash Chandra. *D.H. Lawrence's Novels: A New Historical Approach.* New Delhi: Atlantic, 2009.

Rai, Sudha. *V.S. Naipaul.* Gulab Vaziram for Arnold Heinemann, 1982.

Ray, Mohit K. ed. *V.S. Naipaul: Critical Essays.* Vol. III. New Delhi: Atlantic Publishers, 2005.

Rushdie, Salman. *Imaginary Homelands.* Penguin Books, 1992.

Said, Edward. *Reflections on Exile, and Other Literary and Cultural Essays.* New Delhi: Penguin Books, 2001.

Sharma, S.S. "Identity and Sensuality in *V.S. Naipaul's Half a Life*" in *V.S. Naipaul: An Anthology of Recent Criticism,* Ed. Purabi Panwar. Delhi: Pencraft International, 2007, 173-78.

Singh, M.I. *The Poetics of Alienation and Identity: V.S. Naipaul and George Lamming.* Delhi: Ajanta Books International, 1998.

Trivedi, Harish and Minakshi Mukherjee, eds. *HAS*, Shimla, 1996, reprint, 2000, 56.

Abbreviations

HL	:	*Half a Life*
MAS	:	*Magic Seeds*
LO	:	*Literary Occasion*

12
Indian Diaspora: Old and New

Awanish Rai

With the arrival of the Italian navigator working for the Spanish crown Christopher Columbus in Americas in the year 1492 and of the Portuguese explorer and navigator Vasco da Gama in India in May 1498 the process of exchange of ideas, trade and labour began. Though we have evidences of such exchanges even of the ages earlier to that, in order to make a pinpointed study of the subject called diaspora I shall avail of these dates as significant points of departure not because they have been referred to as a sort of discovery in the history books (not only of Europe but also of even India until recently!) but because they in a way initiate so many of such processes that directly affect the history of the modern world. These 'discoveries of the routes' enamoured the Western world so much so that it could easily be compared to the contemporary human aspirations of exploring the possibilities of life on the planets other than the earth. It opened up the gates on various new worlds: worlds of ideas, trade and commerce, worlds full of ample natural resources and endless possibilities and also the worlds to be subjugated. The process (especially in case of India) that began with the merchandise of spices finally ended up with the trade of human beings. Diasporic population is a living legend to this whole affair.

By quoting Derek Walcott's 1992 Nobel lecture Satendra Nandan in his article entitled "The Diasporic Consciousness: From Biswas to Biswasghat" tries to problematize the diasporic consciousness that has been equated by the former with the consciousness of the person who does not only gather the broken pieces of a vase to remake it but also fights to seal it with so much care that the marks of seal may never be detected by an onlooker. This is precisely a rarely paradoxical situation where one in fact wrestles to achieve the impossible. But an equally significant realization that both Walcott in his lecture and Nandan in his commentary on the same also highlight is the realization of being a part of that "epical celebration of the very essence of human migration" (2000: 50) that grants the mender a greater liberating spatial liberty than the chief participant himself as it connects him to the larger though partially remembered past. While talking specifically about the first generation indentured labourers who embarked on an uncharted voyage in the most unceremonious manner from "the landlocked villages of India to the islands of the Caribbean sea" (2000: 49) in the mid-nineteenth century the first thing that comes to our mind is that they certainly did not move out as the clean slate but rather as the bundle of fragmented but unassailable memories that though further got diluted and deregulated by the cruel presence of the thoroughly inhuman conditions prevailing there, could not really deter them from the herculean task of preserving and promoting them. It was no doubt, a tough task to shoulder their hyphenated identities all the time as one of the major diasporic critics of Indian descent Vijay Mishra puts it in his article entitled "New Lamps for Old: Diasporas Migrancy Border":

> Centres and peripheries—motherlands and diasporas—thus enter into relationships of mutual reinforcement as well as uncanny displacements. This hawker-like capacity to canny one's ancestral baggage around, this capacity for respatialization, however, needs to be tempered by an account of the strong reverse millenarian trend, the double consciousness, of the old Indian diaspora. (2000: 78)

This was perhaps one of the most vicious events ever recorded in the pages of human history when innocent people were permanently banished from their homelands as the punishment for the crime of being poor and of being the natives of a slave nation. People who left their homelands in search of better prospects and better life were never made aware of the fact that they would never ever be able to come back and be reunited with their families, friends and relatives. No doubt, they have been given the choice to return once their contracts got expired but it was no more than a joke asking people to manage their return journey on their own when most of them did not have the required amount to do so. Most of them, therefore, decided to stay on. Moreover no one can question their integrity and devotion as they did not only work hard for the lands where they were taken to but preserved everything that they could take along from India and religiously handed that over to the next generation also.

What Walcott suggests by comparing their ambition to that of the one who gathers up the broken pieces of the vase immediately provides the discourse a metaphorical status as it does not only bring into focus the idealized notion of the nation/homeland but also projects the more vibrant sites of contestation that propose to deliberate upon the still continuing epic battle to exist in a land far away from the homeland. Naipaul's non-fictional prose works on India, apart from being a direct critical commentary on the contemporary state of affairs, are also the sufficient proof of a diasporan's outright rejection of the real as compared to the "imaginary homeland". The image of the homeland that had been passed on to the next generation must have been recreated with a lot of exaggeration mainly for three reasons: one, the first generation was awfully afflicted of nostalgia, the impending dangers of becoming rootless and the endless fears for the generations to come; two, the anxiety to rear the next generation in such a manner that they might not be treated as foreigners in their own homeland, if at all they get a chance to go back; and three, the texts that reached that part of the world with them mostly presented India as an ideal nation that could boast of having once fondled in its bosom the best of human virtues. In such conditions the writers/creative artists had to play a vital role not only by re-creating all that which were once their own but also by highly qualified people. Now the question again was the same: why were they leaving their homeland? And the answer was also the same, i.e. in search of better prospects and better life but what made all the difference was that they, in majority of the cases, were leaving their homeland now on their own conditions. But quite a significant semblance between these two phases is the way people belonging to both of them still hanker for their homeland, feel nostalgic and also suffer the pangs of alienation more or less the same way. Shiva Kumar Srinivasan has a very significant reason to offer:

> The significance of the South Asian Diaspora also lies in the rather unique way in which it intersects with the American Dream.... Why is it that Indians who are comfortable with hyphenated identities and trilingual situations in the subcontinent are unable to overcome the trauma of not being accepted as all-American? (2001: 55)

They went out to contribute in the American Dream project that assured in the first place to treat everyone at par with each other and the government, no doubt, always showed its inclination to implement it but no one can deny the fact that the cases of racial conflicts also increase everyday. It is largely due to this that the diasporic population does not wish to erase all that form part of their collective racial memory nor are they willing to let the next generations forget about it. This is perhaps the most relevant lesson that the Jewish diaspora that has now earned an almost archetypal status in the discourse, has taught to its successors.

It is imperative now to chart out the process of dispersal of Indian population. It began and continued, as we had seen, in two distinct phases. The first phase dispersal marks the height of imperialism and was born out of the earnest need to supply the cheap labour to those newly conquered lands where prospects of fanning were rich. These sugarcoated displacements of the mid-nineteenth century led people from different pans of India to the strange lands across seven seas. The second phase diaspora that gained noticeable acceleration in the later half of the twentieth century was born out of the personal zeal of an individual or a family to lead a more prosperous and a more comfortable life. It was a byproduct of late capitalism and the democratic reforms that were out to reframe international relations and also to further trigger the flow of labour; though, this time, the skilled labour! Although there are numerous differences between the two phases ranging from the mode of dispersal, condition of the first generation diasporic population, reception in the host society to the intensity of cultural alienation, some of them can be counted as follows:

> The first and the most basic difference between the two lies in the way this whole process of dispersal took place. The first phase relied on seductive falsehood, on projecting the wrong notion about the unseen and was therefore a forced act whereas in the second phase of diaspora the decision of leaving the motherland is voluntary and deliberate and should therefore be considered a planned move be built up. The desire to build a house did not only match the very first desire of the earliest human being on earth who aimed at protecting him/herself against the unforeseeable odds of the seasons but it also had to build something that could match the thoroughly coloured blueprint of the collective memory. It is definitely not an exaggeration to find Mr. Biswas wrestling for a house of his own for so long!

Another aspect of life that has an undeniable bearing on an individual's life and personality and that also furthers one's struggle to sustain one's identity are one's food habits. It still remains 'an area of darkness' in the scholarship on Indian diaspora and deserves more survey and further research. Food habits in general parlance keep a person's identity intact till s/he is deliberately willing to change it on his/her own as is witnessed in the case of the pioneering Indian English prose writer Nirad C. Chaudhuri who always objected to the habit of Indians writing in English while preferring at the same time to palate the Indian dishes. But taken otherwise, food habits generally stand for a person's identity and speak volumes about his/her personality. A recent Hindi movie *Bajarangi Bhaijaan* can be an iconoclastic illustration to this effect in which a deaf and dumb girl is ultimately identified by mainly three signifiers: her food habits, mode of prayer and cheers for the cricket team of the country of her birth. This film can be an extremely remarkable heuristic reading on the issue of identity and can also be treated as a wonderful cultural text as to how the secrets of her identity and location are revealed step-by-step. Diasporic population has also kept its food habits intact even after a lapse of more than a century. Vijay Mishra has summarily touched upon this aspect of diasporic life in his aforementioned article:

> Since food rations on the sugar plantations were identical for all indentured labourers, food linked the old Indian diaspora from Surinam to Mauritius to Fiji. The weekly ration was made up of rice, dhal, sugar, tea, dried fish, atta (shaips), salt, oil and half a pound (about 250 grams) of mutton.... Even though linguistic homogeneity (in the indentured diaspora everyone spoke a version of the dialect Bhojpuri at one stage) is no longer a unifying characteristic of this diaspora, food certainly is. (2000: 74)

He then provides a table of daily meals and also the way they were cooked and consumed. He finds these food habits to be a unifying link among the people of old diaspora and also with their lost homeland. Certain significant cultural commodities such as music, dance forms and films also have not only helped retain the link of the diaspora with the motherland but have also paved way for the emergence of various new genres.

Although the second phase diaspora has been continuing since the very beginning of the twentieth century, it was only after the sixth decade of the last century that the number aggressively increased. This massive growth in number was later on popularly called the 'brain drain' for the people who were now out to choose their new centres were most of them. The target destinations of the people belonging to the first phase were literally unknown, unseen and unexplored whereas the second phase diasporans knew the places, have seen and explored them beforehand through various media.

The first phase diasporans were forced to work as indentured labourers on the fields and therefore constituted a marginal section of the host society and remained in the more or less same condition until slavery was completely obliterated from the face of earth whereas the diasporans of the post mid-twentieth century were, most of them, skilled, techno-savvy people who either ran their own ventures or assumed offices of prominence and therefore, mostly, continue to hold affluent positions in the land of migration.

The first phase diasporans were taken to the places where they had to struggle for even sparse basic amenities that are considered essential for human life whereas the second phase diasporans had gone to the places of their choice, the places that offered much better and far more facilities than that could be offered by their places of birth.

The first phase diasporans had to work intensely at least for a century to make those places worth living whereas the second phase migrants had no such struggle to carry forward.

The first generation of the first phase emigrants, most of them being either illiterate or less educated, had also to fight among with themselves against all those that were contained in their racial memories though it was soon ultimately sorted out as Vijay Mishra puts it:

> The ship, the medium of mercantile capitalism, is the first of the cultural units in which social relations were re-sited and renegotiated. In the case of the old Indian diaspora, it produced a site in which caste purities were largely lost (after all the crossing of the dark ocean, the *kalapani,* signified the loss of caste) as well as a new form of socialization that went by the name of *jahajibhai* (ship-brotherhood). (2000: 74)

First generation of the second phase migrants, on the other hand, had nothing much in common for neither did they travel together nor did they reach the same shore: they went away in different hours, by different modes and for different reasons. All of them had their own different stories to tell. Moreover they had, in general, a quiet stay barring their own anxiety and restlessness (which, again in degrees, differed from person to person) to handle the culture shock and a few cases of racial discrimination. But with the passage of time, say, after a lapse of about fifty years or so these cases of racial atrocities have enormously grown in number whether it is in Australia, Canada, England or the USA. Increase in the number of cases of racial atrocities can be taken to be a common phenomenon with the people belonging to both the phases of diaspora and the reason why this is growing everyday is also the same: emergence of the emigrants as the politically powerful pockets. The two coups in Fiji and attacks on students and places of worship are the ample proof of that.

In order to keep their cultural identities intact the first phase migrants had to rely on certain meager texts and articles that they could sail with whereas the second phase migrants has/had everything available at their fingertips. So the kind of wholehearted engagement with the conservation and promotion of the symbols of cultural identity that could help them reclaim and reproduce that which had eventually been lost is certainly not a crisis that could be witnessed with the same intensity among the second phase emigrants.

Whereas the first phase diasporans are a living legend to the episodes of history that are replete with the narratives of abduction, invasion, cruelty, height of colonialist zeal and imperialist ambitions and so on. The second phase diasporans stand as the precursors of a new band of global communities that demonstrates its faith in and upholds the ideals of a global culture.

Whereas the first phase is credited, in whatsoever circumstances and for whatsoever reasons, to have begun the process of hybridity at mass level in the modern times, the second phase demonstrates its urge to accept it as an inevitable condition.

The last and the most significant of all the distinctions counted so far is the issue that considerably and directly affected the expression of the authors belonging to these phases. It is an all time existentialist question of choice: who between the two had the option to return? The first phase diasporans had no choice but to remain in the land where they were deported to while the second phase diasporic population is not only in the constant touch with their families, friends and relatives but are also free to return whenever they like. For a student of literature, it carries a lot of weight as it makes a thoroughly contextualized study of the texts a prerequisite and also provides an invincible insight into the workings of the disparate diasporic minds. The major concerns of diasporic literature pertaining to the themes of alienation, nostalgia, repercussions of exclusivist politics tendencies in the host societies mostly depend on whether one has to/has the option to return or not. The kind of alienation that the first phase diasporans experienced was not simply depressing but frightening also as they did not have the leisure to muse over what was lost but instead had to struggle against all sorts of odds to survive.

There is no doubt about the fact that the Indian diasporas of both the phases have produced many eminent creative writers and critics who are credited to have contributed significantly in the making of the contemporary world literature. But while dealing with the individual authors belonging to either of the two we are mostly prone to pass a judgment on them while treating them at par with one another. Alienation of the first phase is certainly not the alienation of the second, nor are the nostalgic reverberations. Satendra Nandan, in the same aforementioned article, while commenting on the multilayered experiential and spatial concerns of one of the most representative authors of Indian diaspora, V.S. Naipaul, finally concludes that "the betrayal of history is the central philosophical concern of all his (Naipaul's) writing" (2000: 55). This statement explains the specific case of the first phase diaspora but can in no way, by any stretch of imagination, ever be used to refer to the concerns of the whole gamut of writing in general. One more interesting development that can be witnessed is the slow but easily discernible process of the erosion of these lines of demarcation by the mass migration of the people belonging to the first phase diaspora to the same centres where the second phase Indian diasporans are already stationed.

Works Cited

Chakrabarty, Dipesh. "Postcoloniality and the Artifice of History: Who Speaks for 'Indian' Pasts?" in *Contemporary Postcolonial Theory* ed. Padmini Mongia, New Delhi: OUP, 2000.

Jain, Jasbir. "The New Parochialism: Homeland in the Writing of the Indian Diaspora" in *In Diasporas: Theories, Histories, Texts* ed. Makarand Paranjape. New Delhi: Indialog Pub. Pvt. Ltd., 2001.

Mishra, Vijay. "New Lamps for Old: Diasporas Migrancy Border" in *Interrogating Post-colonialism Theory, Text and Context* ed. Harish Trivedi and Meenakshi Mukherjee. Shimla: HAS, 2000.

Nandan, Satendra. "The Diasporic Consciousness: From Biswas to Biswasghat" in *Interrogating Post-colonialism Theory, Text and Context* ed. Harish Trivedi and Meenakshi Mukherjee. Shimla: HAS, 2000.

Srinivasan, Shiva Kumar. "Diaspora and its Discontents" in *In Diasporas: Theories, Histories, Texts* ed. Makarand Paranjape. New Delhi: Indialog Pub. Pvt. Ltd., 2001.

13

Meteoric Identity and Transcultural Experiences of Indian Diaspora in Jhumpa Lahiri's *Unaccustomed Earth*

Ashutosh Singh

The present paper attempts to analyze the issue of diaspora from the perspective of the Indian immigrants' struggle to maintain their identity, i.e. meteoric identity (my own term). It seeks to explore how the Indian experience in America and the conflict between the traditions of her homeland and the culture of her adopted country is the focus of Jhumpa Lahiri in the *Unaccustomed Earth*. It also codifies the finding that the American-Indian relationship is a two-way cultural equation and the Indians who make their homes in the United States are freed of many of the structures created by their homeland's complex, social and cultural codes. As an Indian diasporic writer, Jhumpa Lahiri strives for her native identity and simultaneously endeavours to evolve a new identity in adopted Anglo-American cultural landscape. However, in this clash of cultures, she faces an immigrant's dislocation and displacement. She regards dislocation as a permanent condition of human existence. Hence her sense of belonging to a particular place and culture and at the same time being an 'outsider' to it creates an inner tension in her characters. The diasporic representation and the lived experiences of women diaspora of different generations in the era of globalization proclaim new value and identities in Indian English fiction to attain diasporic voice and identity distinguishable from male writers. These women diasporic writers are attempting to re-write remember rediscover their own perspective and female sensibility.

Every diasporic writer feels the impulse to take a literary journey back home towards "history", towards "past", juggling the double vision of both, a looking forward and a yearning backward. In this act of tight-rope walking, the immigrant writer coalesces the responsibility of transmitting the "accumulative scraps, patches and rags of past" studding them in the frame of the future. This ignites a very significant debate with respect to diasporic situation where there is always juxtaposition between "here" and "there". The diasporic persona attempts to shuttle between two worlds of nativity and immigration in search of a concrete identity. If on one hand there is need to retain features from the homeland, then on the other hand there are overtly deliberate attempts to seek acceptance or assimilation in the new culture. It is this paradox that urges a diasporic writer to recurrently analyse his relationship with his roots because for Jhumpa Lahiri assimilation of the new world does not mean a denial of the past, in fact, a knowledge of one's roots is essential for an autonomous sense of selfhood. M.G. Vassanji says in this context of an immigrant writer: "This reclamation of the past is the first serious act of writing. Having reclaimed it, having given himself a history, he liberates himself to write about the present" (63). Therefore such creative expressions involving their native nations function as bulwark for diasporic writers and save them from the chaos about their identity that may descend upon them.

Frantz Fanon advocates in *The Wretched of the Earth,* that the past should not be acclaimed at the cost of present and future, that the new 'man' cannot be built from the clippings of European historical traditions. That this 'new man' should be capable of enacting a history of decisions, of building a policy of identities cannot be determined by domicile and ethnicity alone. In fact identities are now defined by geographical, lexical, political and cultural differences, as exhibited by diasporic writers who owing to their various kinds of displacements and alien contexts redefine and newly construct alternative identities and communities. The present-day technology of communications and the increasing transnational flow of capital, the geographical distances are not what they were. Rather, now it is far more convenient to retain the consciousness of national origins. The collaboration and coalitional ties, today, with one's native land are neither limiting nor restrictive, but rather profiteering. As Fanon tells us, "The consciousness of self is not the closing of a door to communication. Philosophic thought teaches us, on the contrary, that it is its guarantee. National Consciousness, which is not nationalism, is the only thing that will give us an international dimension" (247). And that is why in literature produced by new immigrants, the 'national consciousness' is prevalent. In the present context, when facets of culture and identity are after self-consciously selected syncretised and elaborated from more than one heritage, it becomes necessary to emphasise the specificity of national identity. Hence, in the context of neo-colonialism and globalisation the position of an immigrant intellectual becomes far more productive and loaded with a greater degree of responsibility. According to Ruben Rumbaut, what is commonly accepted as belonging to the first generation are "persons born and socialized in another country who immigrate as adults" (1165), while the second generation "refers to the U.S.-born and U.S.-socialized children of foreign-born parents, although under this rubric immigration scholars also often...lump together foreign born persons, who immigrated as children" (1165).

Lahiri, one of the major writers of Indian Diaspora, has changed citizenships and lived in various cultural milieus with the disorienting rapidity. The word "diaspora" comes from Greek words for "across" and "to sow or scatter seeds," and it normally refers to "people who have been dislocated from their native homeland through the movements of migration, immigration, or exile" (Braziel and Mannur 1). The human condition is no longer defined in the humanities by traditional identity markers like nationality, origin, settlement, dwelling, roots, birthplace or bloodlines. Ulrich Beck sees this as a long overdue rectification of a fundamental epistemological error in human thinking where such notions of fixed identities and relations caused "the global historical norm of the permeation and intermingling of cultures" to be "falsely portrayed as the exception" or "completely erased from our consciousness" (Qtd. in *Migration Literature and Hybridity* 2). Now an advanced understanding of what it is to be human is allegedly expressed in the figure of the migrant, "the 'borderline' figure of a massive historical displacement", as described by Homi Bhabha, a figure who is supposed to be in a state of uprooted, nomadic, transnational and transcultural fluidity (320). "We pretend that we are trees and speak of roots", says Salman Rushdie. "Look under your feet. You will not find gnarled growths sprouting through the soles. Roots...are a conservative myth, designed to keep us in our places" (85-86). Robin Cohen summarizes the diasporic imagination as a nostalgic trope:

> Diaspora signified a collective trauma, a banishment, where one dreamed of home but lived in exile...all diasporic communities settled outside their natal (or imagined natal) territories, acknowledging the 'old country'—a notion often buried deep in language, religion, custom and folklore—always has some claim on their loyalty and emotion. (ix)

Not only do Indians abroad become diasporic, novelist Amitav Ghosh writes, and not only does India maintain a close relationship with its diaspora, having "no vocabulary for separating the migrant from India," but also "the culture seems to be constructed around the proliferation of differences [...]. To be different in a world of differences is irrevocably to belong" (78), but, argues postcolonial theorist R. Radhakrishnan, to belong in a diasporic sense. The nation form, and particularly India, is "internally heterogenized, 'diasporized' from within," and thus location replaces "home":

> ...the very idea of a proper and non-contingent home in the diaspora is fundamentally contradictory. For after all, what is the diaspora if not the denaturalization of "home" by the concept of "location"? Caught up in a constitutive "between-ness," the diaspora imagines home in opposition to discourses of ontological authenticity and domestic propriety. It is precisely to the extent that home is not natural that the diaspora is able to perform and inaugurate its representations of home as radical and incorrigible "lack".

Lahiri's second collection of short stories *Unaccustomed Earth* is autobiographical and frequently draws upon her own experiences as well as those of her parents, friends, acquaintances, and others in the Bengali communities with which she is familiar. Lahiri places struggles, anxieties, and biases under her microscope so as to better chronicle the nuances and details of immigrant psychology and behaviour. No gesture, no sorrow is spared in her examinations. In all the stories Lahiri applies the metaphor based on the epigraph from Nathaniel Hawthorne's "The Custom-House" which reads: "Human nature will not flourish any more than a potato, if it be planted and replanted, for too long a series of generations, in the same worn-out soil. My children have had other birthplaces, and, so far as their fortunes may be within my control, shall sterile their roots into unaccustomed earth" (ix). Hawthorne suggests that transplanting people into new soil of unaccustomed earth makes them flourish better as they become hardier. All the stories deal with the theme of uprooting and assimilation with efforts made to establish connectivity among characters. Until Unaccustomed Earth, her concerns were confined, for the most part, to Indian immigrants to America and their struggle to raise a family in a country very different from theirs. She wrote about first-generation immigrant parents' struggles to keep their children acquainted with Indian culture and traditions. She wrote about how the parents struggle to keep their children close to them even after they have grown up in order to hang on to the Indian tradition of a joint family, where the parents, their children and the children's family live under the same roof. In the present collection, she moves on to a scrutiny of the fate of the second and third generations. As succeeding generations become increasingly assimilated into Western culture and are comfortable in constructing global perspectives, Lahiri's fiction shifts to the needs of the individual. We see more clearly the departure of the second and following generations from the constraints of their parents. The latter were especially devoted to community and their responsibility to other immigrants; in *Unaccustomed Earth*, there is a departure from the original ethos, and Lahiri's characters embark on paths marked by alienation and self-obsession. In *Unaccustomed Earth*, the writer makes her observations of the second generation Indian Americans absorbed into the Western milieu, yet experiencing deep sense of isolation and alienation. The story deals with the theme of uprooting and assimilation with efforts made to establish connectivity among the characters. Lahiri herself speaks of the eroding cultural links in diaspora creating problems of identity.

> Some of the culture goes by the wayside, or the links is never made. I was aware of that myself when I had my kids. I really felt a sense that I was the end of a line, and that it was a very short line. I knew my parents had parents and so on, but to me, the universe was my parents had they were the far end and I was the near end. There were certain intensities to the experience of that first generation and their offspring that don't carry over. I'm very aware of my parents' experience, how I grew up, and now how my children are growing up. There is such a stark difference in those two generations. (Bookforum April/May 08)

In the title story "Unaccustomed Earth", Ruma is a post-immigrant, who is struggling to maintain an equal footing with her family and the world outside. Settled in Seattle with an American husband, Adam, and a son, Akash, Ruma seems to have disguised herself completely in the American way. But it is through her late mother's memories and her father that she struggles to re-establish contacts with her roots. As a child, Ruma and her brother Romi are forcibly taken to India to visit their grandparents. Her mother seems to have "lived for these journeys" (8). Viewing the gradual segregation of his children from their ethnic origins. Ruma's father tries his best to cover up the fissures that would soon turn into a gorge. "And so they'd gone in spite of the expense, in spite of the sadness he felt each time he returned to Calcutta, in spite of the fact that the older his children grew, the less they wanted to go" (8). Ruma's mother sticks to wearing "her brightly coloured saris, her dime-sized maroon bindi, her jewels" (11). She is strict enough with Ruma "so much so that Ruma had never spoken to her in English" (12). It is due to her mother's influence that Ruma can speak Bengali exclusively in the initial years of her life. But being the child of America, "Bengali had never been a language in which she felt like an adult. Her own Bengali was slipping from her" (12). Therefore, she can't blame her son. Akash for forgetting whatever little Bengali she has taught him. Ruma's mother always laments "the fact that her daughter preferred pants and skirts to the clothing she wore, that there would be no one to whom to pass on her things" (17). To her parents:

> Ruma seems foreign in every way. The more she grows, more aloof she becomes. When she is young, her parents are her entire world. But eventually that need dissipated, that, dwindled to something amorphous, tenuous, something that threatened at times to snap. That loss was in store for Ruma too; her children would become strangers, avoiding her. (54)

Thus, Ruma's initial relation with her parents is contradictory. It is a clash between solitude and merger. Ruma having successfully merged with the host culture begins to drift away from her ethnic origins.

By the end of the story, Lahiri features the cordial relations that begin to develop between the two generations of immigrants. Ruma and her mother try to attune to each other's lifestyles. But as Helena Grice puts it: "Ethnicity never exists in its 'pure' form because it is always already shaped by the cultural forces surrounding it" (5). Hence, Ruma's mother begins to shed her expatriate garb and put on a multi-cultural mask. Her sudden desire to visit Europe to see "The Canals of Venice or the Eiffel Tower or the windmills and tulips of Holland" (19), surprised the entire family because "it had been an unquestioned fact that visiting family in Calcutta was the only thing worth boarding a plane for" (19).

Ten years back, Ruma's mother tried everything to take Ruma out of her marriage to Adam, "saying that he would divorce her.... 'You are ashamed of yourself, of being Indian, that is the bottom line'" (26), her mother tells Ruma time and again. But soon she accepts her American son-in-law and denies all her previous objections:

> She grew to love Adam as a son, a replacement for Romi, who had crushed them by moving abroad and maintaining

> only distant ties. Her mother would chat with Adam on the phone, even when Ruma was not at home, e-mailing him from time to time, carrying on a game of scrabble with him over the Internet. (26)

It is after the birth of Akash that Ruma's relationship with her mother becomes harmonious. A grandchild seems to rejuvenate in Ruma's mother:

> For the first time in her life Ruma felt forgiven for the many expectations she'd violated or shirked over the years.... Her mother had even begun to exercise, getting up at five in the morning, wearing an old Colgate Sweatshirt of Ruma's. She wanted to live to see her grandchildren married. (27)

It is, ironically, the third generation immigrant, Akash who acts as a bridge between the mother and the daughter (i.e. the first and second generation immigrants). "Oddly it was his [her] grandson, who was only half-Bengali to begin with, who did not even have a Bengali surname, with whom he [she] felt a direct biological connection, a sense of himself [herself] reconstituted in another" (54).

The change in Uma's mother is an evidence of the transformation of cultural heterogenization into cultural homogenization. The global phenomenon of cultural compression causes the creation of a hybrid identity. Thus, Uma's mother adopts a new identity in order to fit well within the mosaic of multiple cultures. In an interview to Newsweek. Lahiri admits "The ink hasn't dried yet on our lives here" (Patel 80). Being a second generation immigrant herself. Lahiri confesses that diasporic characters like her cannot overcome their past. The multi-cultural situation doesn't allow the past to be wiped out completely. The past does have an impact on their present, however slight it may be. As a result, Ruma a second generation immigrant, witnesses a gradual sublimation of the mental, cultural and native differences between her parents and herself. The differences she once considered to be gigantic begin to evaporate as she comes to realize the realities of two cultures co-existing in and around her. After her mother's death:

> Ruma feared that her father would become a responsibility, an added demand, continuously present in a way she was no longer used to. It would mean an end to the family she'd created on her own: herself and Adam and Akash,... she couldn't imagine tending to her father as her mother had, serving the meals her mother used to prepare. (7)

But over the years, she notices how self-sufficient, helpful, caring and adjustable her father has become. As a result, she requests him to start living with her family in Seattle. "He knew that it was not for his sake that his daughter was asking him to live here. It was for hers. She needed him, as he'd never felt she'd needed him before, apart from the obvious things he provided her in the course of his life" (53). Thus, we see a bond beginning to develop between the first and the second generation immigrants.

Though Ruma appears to be a thorough American in as far as her language, clothing, eating habits and attitude are concerned, yet she doesn't want her son Akash to be an American child. "In spite of her efforts he was turning into the sort of American child she was always careful not to be, the sort that horrified and intimidated her mother: imperious, afraid of eating things" (23). When young, Ruma usually corrects the English of her father, feeling irritated. But now, she ignores her father's linguistic errors, because she understands the fact that the adopted land and its language can never become inherent as the motherland or mother tongue. We thus witness a confluence, when the older generation advances in thought towards multicultural ism and the younger generation retreats by adopting some ethnic values.

The story "Hell-Heaven" is about the conflict between Aparna, called Boudi, and her daughter Usha. Aparna, being the first generation immigrant, continues to cling to her Bengali ways. She wears "the red and white bangles unique to Bengali married women, and a common Tangail Sari, and had a thick stem of vermilion powder in the center parting of her hair" (61). She stays home all day and her only job is to cook and clean for her family. She expects Usha to speak only Bengali at home. She dislikes Deborah, the American fiancee of Pranab Chakraborty; because she secretly covets Pranab. She doesn't reveal her love for Pranab because she doesn't want to break the Bengali code of a loyal and sincere wife. Her hatred for Deborah is rooted in their ethnic differences.

> It was universally agreed that she [Deborah] had stripped Pranab Kaku not only of his origins but of his independence. She was the enemy, he was her prey, and their example was invoked as a warning, and as vindication that mixed marriages were a doomed enterprise. (75)

Usha manages to live an American life despite the cultural and ethnic values enforced upon her by Aparna. Usha feels that English is the language in which she can express herself freely. Deborah's visits produce contrasting impacts on Usha as compared to Aparna. Usha begins to anticipate Deborah's visits. She develops a connection with Deborah which she feels lies deep within their American origin. Being born and brought up in America, Usha considers herself to be as American:

> With Deborah I had a companion. She knew all about the books I read, about Pippi Long-Stocking and Anne of Green Gables, she gave me the sorts of gifts my parents had neither the money nor the inspiration to buy.... I felt protective of her, aware that she was unwanted, that she was resented, aware of the nasty things people said. (70)

According to Bhabha, the kinship that develops between Usha and Deborah is the result of an encounter with alien identities:

> Each time the encounter with identity occurs at the point at which something exceeds the frame of the image, it eludes the eye, evacuates the self as site of identity and autonomy and—most important—leaves a resistant trace, a stain of the subject, a sign of resistance. We are no longer confronted with an ontological problem of being but with the discursive strategy of the moment of interrogation, a moment in which the demand for identification becomes, primarily, a response to other questions of signification and desire, culture and politics. (49-50)

Being a second generation immigrant, Usha drifts away from her ethnic origins towards the adopted culture. The land once alien for her parents becomes home for Usha. Deborah is viewed by Usha, as a fellow citizen. "I felt that she understood me better than anyone else in the world" (70). This intimacy between the second generation immigrants with the host subjects is a clear evidence of such immigrants drifting so far away from their roots that they begin to see their ethnic origins to be something exotic. As Usha reaches adolescence, she begins to keep secrets from Aparna. She evader her with the help of her friends:

> When she screamed at me for talking too long on the telephone, or for staying too long in my room, I learned to scream back, telling her that she was pathetic, that she knew nothing about me, and it was clear to us both that I had stopped needing her, definitively and abruptly, just as Pranab Kaku had. (76-77)

The change in Usha's attitude is stimulated by the cultural pressure that Aparna forced on Usha throughout her childhood. This sudden outburst is a revolt against all the ethnic norms that Usha no longer wants to cling to. By the end of the story, Aparna has come to terms with Usha:

> She had accepted the fact that I was not only her daughter but a child of America as well. Slowly, she accepted that I dated one American man, and then another, and then yet another, that I slept with one though we were not married. She welcomed my boyfriends into our home and when things didn't work out she told me I would find someone better. After years of being idle, she decided, when she turned fifty, to get a degree in library science at a nearby university. (81-82)

Thus, we witness that it is Aparna who succumbs to the alien lifestyle in order to harmonize with Usha, a second generation immigrant. The first generation immigrants, therefore, have to surrender to the adopted culture in order to maintain kinship with their further generations.

The story "Only Goodness" portrays the life of Sudha and her constant conflict with her parents. Having worked with a large number of second generation immigrants, Uma Parameswaran states:

> I am aware of the vast differences between their attitudes to "home" and their parents. While many have felt the

> stings of racism in their school environment, most choose the survival technique of downplaying it. Often this works to their advantage because both oppressor and victim outgrow their roles; but some of the victims carry the scars of trauma all their lives. (Parameswaran 36)

Sudha is one such immigrant, whose brother's birth rekindles the harsh childhood memories of Sudha. Sudha doesn't want Rahul's upbringing to be as un-Americanised as her own. "Even as an adult, she wished only that she could go back and change things: the ungainly things she'd worn, the insecurity she'd felt, all the innocent mistakes she'd made" (187). As a result, she takes charge of Rahul's upbringing. She buys him the right toys, the right story books, the right Halloween costumes. "She had slipped through the cracks, but she was determined that her little brother should leave his mark as a child in America" (136). She also begins to envy him "because people could call him Rahul, that he could introduce himself in crowds without questions" (136-37). Sudha has no fondness for her childhood because it seems limited to the ethnic code of conduct that her parents adhered to at that time. But in case of Rahul, "Sudha supposed it was a combination of his being a boy and being younger, and her parents being more at ease with the way things worked in America by then" (137).

Sudha's submissive attitude soon takes form of a revolt:

> Sudha had waited until college to disobey her parents. Before then she had lived according to their expectations, her persona scholarly, her social life limited to other demure girls in her class, if only to ensure that one day she would be set free. (29)

It is Sudha who later introduces her brother to alcohol, a practice strictly denied by her parents. But when her mother comes to know of Rahul's addiction, she doesn't want to blame her son.

> Sudha pitied her mother, pitied her refusal to accommodate such an unpleasant and alien fact, her need to blame America and its laws instead of her son.... Her parents had always been blind to the things that plagued their children:

> being teased at school for the color of their skin or for the funny things their mother occasionally put into their lunch boxes.... "Depression" was a foreign word to them, an American thing. (143)

Sudha's parents don't want to accept the fact that the identities of their children have been polluted by the foreign influence.

Without any protest they accept Sudha's decision to marry Roger, who is fourteen years older to Sudha and is previously married. "Sudha felt that they were not so much making room for Roger in the family as allowing him to take her away" (152). Their quiet approval of Roger is just another effort of Sudha's parents to preserve the relationship with their daughter. "Sudha regarded her parent's separation from India as an ailment that ebbed and flowed like a cancer" (138). This ailment has no permanent cure. The only remedy is to restructure the linguistic, cultural and traditional aspects of their identity in accordance with the foreign values.

Rahul's failure to fulfill the American Dream is the result of the conflicting position he has found himself in. Like Ruma from "Unaccustomed Earth" he is a hybrid, and in the same way he finds it distressing to live in-between two cultures, his alcoholism being a symbolic expression of distress. Neither he nor his parents accept his border position; while he wishes to live like an American, they want him to preserve the Indian way of life, yet take advantage of opportunities that America offers, such as excellent education and job. They still separate the two worlds, India and America, creating paradoxical situations: on the one hand they want to think their children live an idyllic life in the American Paradise, free from the burden of the Indian past as the narrator comments:

> In their opinion their children were immune from the hardships and injustices they had left behind in India, as if the inoculations the pediatrician had given Sudha and Rahul when they were babies guaranteed them an existence free from suffering. (144)

On the other hand, they resist the idea that their children come in contact with and therefore might be influenced by American reality: "'depression' was a foreign word to them, an American thing" (143-44). That is why they do not acknowledge Rahul's problem. Rahul is suspended between the strains put on by his Indian parents and his already acquired Americanness. The Indian way of life pressed upon him by his parents stifles his American spirit of individualism, desire for freedom and self-fulfillment, expressed by his wish to engage in artistic activity and other attempts of breaking away from the parental control.

Rahul is a dislocated subject. He does not want to identify with his Indian family and Indian way of life. However, when he eventually finds strength in himself to abandon his parents in order to live his own way, the American way with an American girlfriend, he fails. His failure should be read symbolically—as a hybrid, he cannot be the One, or the Other, he cannot live as an American or an Indian. He will not succeed until he agrees to his middle position, his in-betweenness. Only from this position he can start building anew.

Lahiri changes her writing style for the first story, much of which is written in a first person address. The story revolves around two people who, despite being childhood acquaintances and their families being old friends, lead drastically different lives. Two decades after Kaushik's family stays with Hema's as houseguests, they meet again by chance, just days before they are to enter into completely different phases of their lives, and they discover a strong connection with one another. The entire story of "Hema and Kaushik" is divided into three parts—"Once in a Lifetime", "Year's End" and "Going Ashore".

"Once in a Lifetime" is another story of a post-immigrant, Hema, who shares completely different relations with her mother Shibani and her aunt, Mrs. Parul Choudhary, who are both first generation immigrants. Hema is not on cordial terms with her mother Shibani, who is midway through her identity reconstruction; and like an expatriate continues to cling to some shades of her ethnic identity. According to William Safran one of the six features of Diasporas is: "the retention of a collective memory, vision, or myth about the original homeland—its physical location, history, etc." (85). It is this vision of homeland that Shibani is trying to locate in the midst of the alien host culture.

Hema and Shibani contradict each other on petty matters; and it is these slight differences that later form a large gulf never to be overcome:

> My mother considered the idea of a child sleeping alone a cruel American practice and therefore did not encourage it,...she told me that she had slept in the same bed as her parents until the day she was married and that it was perfectly normal. But I knew that it was not normal, not what my friends at school did, and that they would ridicule me if they knew. (229)

Despite Shibani's constant efforts, she cannot instill the Indianness in Hema:

> I found trips to India dull, that I didn't like the geckos that clung to the walls in the evening...or the giant cockroaches that sometimes watched me as I bathed. I didn't like the comments my relatives made freely in my presence. (241)

From the very beginning Hema wants to shed the Indian aspect of her identity and merge completely with America—its culture and lifestyle. On the other hand, Parul's American ways immediately attract Hema. She begins to admire the way Parul is more American than her mother even though she has spent the last six years in India. "Bombay had made them more American than Cambridge had,... There were remarks concerning your mother's short hair, her slacks, the Johnnie Walker she and your father continued to drink after the meal was finished" (235). This is an evidence of globalization along with international standardization. Global interdependence nullifies the boundaries, bringing the world closer; and allowing the cultural influences to seep through.

Parul and her husband, Dr. Chowdhary "enjoyed the change of pace, having mysteriously acquired a taste for things like steak and baked potatoes, while my parents had not" (246). Thus, Hema begins to associate with Parul's immigrant traits. Christine Gomez remarks about immigrants that they are "middleman in more sense than one. They are not only brokers or go betweens in various deals, but people who are in the middle of where action is" (Gomez 139-40). Hema considers Parul to be one such interpreter between two cultures. The reason why Parul leaves India is not for the treatment of cancer but more to be left alone. Hema completely agrees with this thought of Parul not wanting to be suffocated by the attention of people in India. Hema's intimacy with Parul is the consequence of their identities being fluid. The similar trait of acculturation acts as a binding agent between Hema and Parul.

Cultural collision leads to a certain seepage of values and customs which cause cultural contamination. No two cultures in confrontation remain virgin. The alien as well as the host subjects are affected by the cultural dialogue. Thus, it may be concluded that the two simultaneous realities of globalization are cultural fragmentation on one hand and cultural homogenization on the other.

The second story "Year's End," surrounds Kaushik struggling to cope up with his father's remarriage after his mother's death. His frustrations in his relationship with his step-mother (Chitra) and her daughters (Rupa and Piu), exposes his sense of loss and identity. At once his father's detailing out certain information to his unarticulated queries is notable:

> "I don't ask you to care for her, even to like her,".... "You are a grown man, you have no need for her in your life as I do. I only ask, eventually, that you understand my decision".... "They arrive in two weeks. You will see them when you come home for Christmas." (254)

That day when his father called, Kaushik had a girl named Jessica in his bed, who knew nothing of his mother's death or about his father. They had spent only a few weekends together and he had not bothered to tell anything about his family. This sequence brings in the element of free life in diaspora. He recollects how his mother had packed her ruby and pearl to be given to his future wife.

Reaching home to meet his family, Kaushik found shy young girls who were told by their mother to address him Kaushik

Dad. Kaushik went into the kitchen as he used to do in the last days of his mother, trying to do up the work. He went in for the bottle of Scotch his parents used to relish. His father came in to tell him he had stopped taking Scotch giving the excuse that Chitra was rather old fashioned. However, he poured the drink for his father:

> He glanced at Chitra, and after some small silent communication between them she walked out.... "For some time now. Also, I didn't want to alarm Chitra." ".... Instead I said, taking the bottle from his hand, I hope it's all right if I alarm her." "Just be quiet about it, especially around the girls." "...My parents had never been quiet about their fondness for Johnnie Walker, around me, around anyone." (264)

He comes to know that the girls were over protected by their mother as they never went out anywhere without her. Their holding hands together while walking through the parking lot is yet another indication of building warmer relationships: "I felt separate from them in every way but at the same time could not deny the things that bound us together" (272).

Kaushik had his share of Christmas gifts from his father, a sweater, a shirt and $1000 which he felt was too much. His father had also arranged a special trip for the girls to visit Disney World. Though his father invited him to join, he felt it not a convincing invitation. But the girls were keen on having him for the trip:

> sensed that they needed me to guard them, as I needed them, from the growing, incontrovertible fact that Chitra and my father now formed a couple. My presence was proof that my mother had once existed, just as they represented the physical legacy of their dead father. (282)

Observing the two girls look at his mother's photograph in a shoe box makes him fume with anger and in his fury he took all things and drove off in the night and landed in a motel:

> You have no right to be looking at those,.... They don't belong to you, do you understand?... Well, you've seen it for yourselves, how beautiful my mother was.... Your

> mother is nothing in comparison. Just a servant to wash my father's clothes and cook his meals. That's the only reason she's here, the only reason both of you are here. (286-87)

Kaushik kept driving for four days without any map, and was told he would hit Canada. His mental anxiety is symbolically presented through the awe-inspiring landscape:

> The sky was different, without color, taut and unforgiving. But the water was the most unforgiving thing, nearly black at times, cold enough, I knew, to kill me, violent enough to break me apart. The waves were immense, battering rocky beaches without sand. The farther I went, the more desolate it became.... (289-90)

Kaushik reminisces the past when his family lived with Hema's parents. Though he hated to be with them, he now remembers those days with nostalgia: "Though we didn't belong there, it was the last place that had felt like a home" (291). Close to the Canadian border, he found a striking spot where he brought the shoebox of photographs of his mother. Scanning through them he couldn't but think of scattering them. But he desisted the temptation and put them back in the box. It was his symbolic burial of mother's pictured memory in the unaccustomed earth.

In the final story "Going Ashore", Lahiri becomes an omniscient narrator bringing together Kaushik and Hema in Rome after many years of separation. She very artfully brings self-realization in both the protagonists as they get very intimate with each other. But the break in narration comes with Hema taking over in the last portion like a coda.

Hema has come to Rome as a Latin professor at Wellesley, taking advantage of a colleague's apartment in the Ghetto. Neither her parents nor her would-be husband Navin knew what she was doing in Rome. She merely called it a visiting lectureship at the institute of classical studies. "Her scholarly life was a mystery to them, something at once impressive and irrelevant. It had earned her a PhD and a tenure-track job" (294). Her friend Giovanna had arranged for her research at the American

Academy. However in October she would take an improvised leave of absence to visit her retired parents in Calcutta, and to get married to Navin in an arranged wed-lock. She had only three weekend contacts with him by e-mail and through occasional phone calls, exchanging words purely out of formality. Navin was a professor of Physics at Michigan State. They were both physically attracted to each other: it would eventually culminate in their life together. In the meantime in Rome, she continued an affair with a former lover Julian to divorce his wife and marry her. Since it didn't happen, they had to separate bitterly.

Still there was something that prevented her from going deeply into any relationship with people. Lahiri deftly comments on her inner conflicts:

> Now she was free of both of them, free of her past and free of her future in a place where so many different times stood cheek by jowl like guests at a crowded party. She was alone with her work, alone abroad for the first time in her life, aware that her solitary existence was about to end. (289)

Now as a professor, having researched on Lucretius, she was soaked in Latin Literature which enabled "her to bring a dead world to life" (299).

Lahiri introduces Kaushik coming to Rome as a photojournalist who had wandered for about twenty years, mostly in Latin America. He had been to war zones of Israel, Guatemala, Mexico, Buenos Aires, Africa and the Middle East, erking out a living by taking pictures of corpses. He had little connection with his family. His father visited him in Rome on their transit to Calcutta. He was planning to move to Asia working for a magazine. For Kaushik, migrant life began from childhood and he "was always happiest to be outside, away from the private detritus of life" (309). His Photojournalism matched his diasporic life:

> He was reminded of his family's moves every time he visited another refugee camp, every time he watched a family combing through rubble for their possessions. In the end, that was life: a few plates, a favorite comb, a pair

> of slippers, a child's string of beads. He wanted to believe that he was different, that in ten minutes he could be on his way to anywhere in the world. But he knew that it was impossible, wherever he landed, not to form attachments. (309)

He became a man from nowhere, devoid of emotional and physical attachment to anyone. What was his identity? His origin didn't matter to him as a photographer, though in Europe he was regarded as an Indian.

Kaushik chanced to meet Hema who remembered their living together when she was thirteen and how she nurtured her longing for him:

> It was unquestioned that they would not part yet, unquestioned that though they had not seen or thought of each other in decades, not sought each other out, something precious had been stumbled upon, a newborn connection that could not be left unattended, that demanded every particle of their care. (311)

He took her to his apartment and that night was one of intimacy between the two. They spent a lot of time together in the night, in out of the way restaurants, bars, and abandoned squares, sitting together like teenaged couple kissing each another:

> It was Hema who stayed awake, listening to him breathing, craving his touch again as light came into the sky. In the morning, looking into the small mirror over the sink in Kaushik's bathroom, she saw that the area around her lips, at the sides of her mouth, was covered with small red bumps. And she was pleased by that unbecoming proof, pleased that already he had marked her. (314)

After travelling together in Italy for some time, both Hema and Kaushik would choose different routes—she would go off to India and Kaushik to Hong Kong. After the last meal together, Kaushik asked her to go with him and refrain from marrying Navin but she was quick to reply, "It's too late" (322).

The story concludes with Hema taking up narration as if to put an end to the story she began, recollecting from her childhood memory. She couldn't just forget the past. She searched for information on Kaushik, to get in touch with him. She surfed his website and found the last images he had posted with the background of the shore scene they had seen from Volterra. "Three blackened faces, supposed to be Etruscan divinities, that loomed over our heads. And then, scenes of another coast. Two children playing, a gentle turquoise sea" (332). It is indicative of migrant spirit as well as emotional rift in relationships that the two have experienced. Now they have to live their lives on different shores, pinning for each other—so close, yet so split apart. Hema returned to her life in Massachusetts thirty years after Kaushik and his parents left for India. The cycle of life is complete: sprouting-blooming-dying—and sprouting again. In February she came to know from an obituary in the *New York Times* that Kaushik was no more. It was a shocking piece of news to her.

Though the story is one of intense love and passion, it does not end in wedding bells. It rather ends in grief, isolation and death. Lahiri has captured the agony of people trying to survive in a situation of having lost familial and cultural relationships due to circumstances in diasporic existence. The stories of Hema and Kaushik are full of pathos ending in unfulfilled love. "Once in a lifetime" can happen to any family in diaspora, leading to establish family ties and growing up in love. The sense of uprooting and being replanted recur in the stories. The breaking point comes with the death of Kaushik's mother. But life must continue with resurgence. In "Year's End" when Kaushik's father marries Chitra, he fails to understand the emotional and physical needs of his father, Chitra and the two young children. Both Kaushik and Hema attempt to feel their own protected worlds. Kaushik's search leads him to globe trotting as a photojournalist, trying to take roots in the unaccustomed earth. Succeeding nowhere, he finds the turning point of his life in the arms of Hema. But that too is shattered, climaxing in his final uprooting from life itself. Life moves on with Hema, though unfulfilled in love, with the foetus growing within her, giving meaning to life through "Going Ashore" to new places.

The diasporic predicament in relationships is well wrought out by the fictionist when she let her protagonists take different roads, quite opposite of those travelled by their immigrant parents. This is where the cultural and familial ties are broken in the unaccustomed earth. They all become strangers in their own worlds and have to fend for their own survival in diaspora as Kaushik experienced. "From childhood, he realized now, he was always happiest to be outside, away from the private detritus of life" (309). Both Hema and Kaushik have to escape their parents' way of life to live in unaccustomed earth, striving to set up homes.

The stories are intense studies of individuals caught in between conflicts of family relationships and cultural traditions. They try to establish their individual identities in a new-milieu, experiencing at the same time the sense of displacement, alienation, and isolation. These individuals, caught up in the confusion of their migrant lives, need to get connected to family and friends for emotional fulfillment. "Hema and Kaushik" stories are a compendium of all Lahiri's ideas and thoughts about life and its intriguing predicaments. Her narration is simple and straightforward for the common reader. At the same time her subtle nuances with psychological undertones, can be brain-teasers for a perceptive critic.

As a contemporary writer of Indian diaspora, Lahiri voices the conflicts of those who have traveled across continents and represents the lives of immigrants who have to deal with the outcomes of the cultural clashes they have to face throughout their lives in their new home. Jhumpa Lahiri, both in her novels (*The Namesake* and *The Lowland*) and in her short stories (*Interpreter of Maladies* and *Unaccustomed Earth*) deals with the search for identity, the issues of alienation and exile and the suspicious way in which Indians eye American culture. Despite their attempts at assimilation, somewhat deep down they remain very Indian, and that is why they end up confused and fragmented. They are not able to belong wholly to either and diaspora's identity is just like the meteor. More than ever before the study of diasporic writing is particularly important in the present circumstances when the act of displacement is gaining enormity multi-dimensionally, when the line between centre and periphery is getting smudged by new interpretations of history. Diasporic writing, especially in the age of globalization, is a consciousness-raising genre, where, political inequality runs alongside themes of nostalgia, imaginative, reconstructions of the homeland, and identities. The theme of identity in diasporic writing is not merely an exercise in exploring multiplicities of location and subject-hoods; it is larger political issue of global justice, cultural rights, self-determination and cosmopolitanism.

Works Cited

Bhabha, Homi K. *The Location of Culture*. London: Routledge, 1994. Print.

Bookforum. "Migration, Assimilation and Inebriation." Jhumpa Lahiri talks with Bookforum. April-May 2008. n.pag. Web. 25 May 2015.

Braziel, Jana Evans and Anita Mannur (eds). *Theorizing Diaspora*. Maiden. MA: Blackwell, 2003. Print.

Cohen, Robin. *Global Diaspora: An Introduction*. Seattle: University of Washington Press, 1997. Print.

Fanon, Frantz. *The Wretched of the Earth*. Trans. Constance Farrington. Harmondsworth: Penguin, 1961. Print.

Ghosh, Amitav. "The Diaspora in Indian Culture." *Public Culture* 2.1 (1989): 73-78. Print.

Lahiri, Jhumpa. *Unaccustomed Earth*. New York: Vintage Books, 2008. Print.

Moslund, Sten Pultz. *Migration Literature and Hybridity: The Different Speeds of Transcultural Change*. Basingstoke: Palgrave Macmillan, 2010. Print.

Radhakrishnan, R. "Adjudicating Hybridity, Co-ordinating Betweenness." *Jouvert* 5.1 (2000): n.pag. Web. 10 May 2015.

Rumbaut, Ruben. "Ages, Life Stages, and Generational Cohorts: Decomposing the Immigrant First and Second Generations in the United States." *IMR* 38.3 (2004): 1160-1205. Print.

Vssanji, M.G. ed. *A Meeting of Streams: South Asian Canadian Literature*. Toronto: TSAR, 1989. Print.

14

India of the Mind: Homeland and Diasporic Contingencies

Namrata Rathore Mahanta

The publication of V.S. Naipaul's *An Area of Darkness* was met with a surge of vitriolic response from all corners of India, the point of departure being the difference between Naipaul's India and the India of his Indian critics. Numerous writers had written about India before Naipaul did, and not always sympathetically. Beverly Nicholas or Catherine Mayo could be ignored because being 'foreigners' they were not expected to have the profundity of vision to comprehend the antithesis that is India. But with Naipaul and his Indian ancestry, Indians felt betrayed. *An Area of Darkness* aroused Indian men of letters into launching counter-attacks on Naipaul and his vision of India. Nissim Ezekiel's essay "Naipaul's India and Mine" is considered to be an integral part of the above-mentioned body of Naipaul criticism. This paper attempts to read Ezekiel's essay as distinct voice of diasporic-reasoning amidst the vast body of Naipaul criticism in India. Further, this paper analyses Ezekiel's attitude as the product of his racial, cultural and linguistic identity and the process of his having come to terms with it. Drawing on his poetry, the paper argues that having undergone phases of protest and acceptance common to the diasporic sensibility, Ezekiel could identify *An Area of Darkness* as a record of Naipaul's loss of his 'idea' of homeland and also anticipates the mutation this 'idea' subsequently underwent twenty-seven years later in Naipaul's *India: A Million Mutinies Now.*

A brief overview of the critique of *An Area of Darkness* reveals that the response to the book is governed by defensive nationalistic sentiments. H.H. Anniah Gowda's reaction to the book is representative of many Indian critics who accuse Naipaul of presenting a partial view of their country: "Naipaul in his personal reminiscences has chosen to shut his eyes to the India which is not defecating" (167). K. Natwar Singh holds: "It is Mr. Naipaul's unique achievement to have passed that amount of time in India without meeting a single worthwhile human being" (35) and C.D. Narasimhaiah while conceding that "our failings are so many and so varied that the most patriotic of us cannot defend them", has charged Naipaul for "blaming us as much for being Indian as for not being wholly Indian" (84, 90). Ezekiel's essay is distinctive because it accommodates difference in perspective and vision and also tries to get at the root of the influences which shape a writer's sensibility. Published in 1965, "Naipaul's India and Mine" is the first critique of Naipaul's *An Area of Darkness,* which locates the dichotomy of alienation and belonging in the sensibility of an uprooted creative artist:

> My quarrel with Mr. Naipaul...is not because of these condemnatory judgements of his.... My quarrel is that Mr. Naipaul...writes exclusively from the point of view of *his own dilemma, his temperamental alienation* from his mixed background, *his choice* and *his escape*...that choice is not open to all, the escape for most is not from the community but into it. (74, emphasis added)

Ezekiel catches Naipaul the person and Naipaul the writer overriding each other's experiences. He points to the subtle ways in which diasporic consciousness works in the interior landscape of the writer's mind. Ezekiel also categorically declares that this work is more a personal account of disappointment. He identifies four keywords which foreground the sensibility of a diasporic writer—"dilemma", "alienation", "background" and "escape". Naipaul's later books have laid bare this progression in the course of his changing vision. In 1987, Naipaul writes in *The Enigma of Arrival*:

> ...the idea given me by my education...was that the writer was a person possessed of sensibility; that the writer was someone who recorded or displayed an inward development.... To be that kind of writer (as I interpreted it) I had to be false; I had to pretend to be other than I was, other than what a man of my background could be. Concealing this colonial—Hindu self below the writing personality. I did both my material and myself much damage. (134)

And again in *Finding the Centre* Naipaul writes:

> To become a writer, that noble thing I had thought it necessary to leave. Actually, to write, it was necessary to go back. It was the beginning of self-knowledge. (40)

It is thus evident that Ezekiel had anticipated this dilemma when he talked of "choice of escape" with reference to Naipaul. In the essay, Ezekiel provides practical interpretations of the incidents described by Naipaul. He declares that he shares most of Naipaul's ideas and problems but has a different vision of India. Thus, the actions of Ramnath, Malhotra, Bunty and others recorded by Naipaul in *An Area of Darkness* acquire a humane dimension in the hands of Ezekiel. He delineates Naipaul's indictment of "a greater philosophy of despair leading to passivity":

> Few Indians are willing to believe that the roots of their failure go deep into history. They believe in their high ideals and attribute failure to not living up to these. That the ideals are false and stultifying is never clearly perceived. Hence the contradiction between words and behaviour which is virtually universal in India the insensitive contradiction between belief and way of life (86). The unique critique of *An Area of Darkness* forwarded by Ezekiel thus raises issues which can be addressed through a comparative study of the growth of these two very different writers. That Ezekiel's critique of Naipaul stems from his sensibility and his insider-outsider duality is reflected in the body of his poetry. Ezekiel's poetry not only encompasses the existential realities of modern urban life but also lays bare

> a process of self-exploration of an individual who lives in borrowed space. Like Naipaul, Ezekiel too faces the predicament of double alienation. While Naipaul rejected his Caribbean roots, and finds himself unable to relate to India, Ezekiel neither anchors on to his Jewish identity nor falls in with the rooted Indian identity: "my background makes me a natural outsider. Circumstances and decisions relate me to India." (88)

Ezekiel's alienation from his own community, is revealed in his poem "Background, Casually":

> At home on Friday nights the prayers
> Were said. My morals had declined I heard of Yoga and of Zen
> Could I, perhaps be rabbi-saint?
> The more I searched, the less I found. (179)

Ezekiel envies Jamini Roy for the rooted style of his paintings:

> He started with a different style
> He travelled so he found his roots
> His rage became a quiet smile
> Prolific in its proper fruits. (125-26)

This journey from "rage" to "quiet smile" is the discovery of a sense of belonging which Ezekiel identifies as lacking in his own case. In the poem "Case Study" written around the same time, Ezekiel voices similar sentiments:

> The pattern will remain unless you break
> It with a sudden jerk; but use your head
> Not all returned as heroes who had fled
> In wanting both to have and eat the cake
> Not all who fail are counted with the fake. (125)

The poem "Enterprise" projects an uneasy equilibrium that has to be consciously achieved by a person who sets out as a seeker:

> When, finally, we reached the place,
> We hardly knew why we were there.

The trip had darkened every face,
Our deeds were neither great nor rare.
Home is where we have to earn our grace. (118)

The poem "A Morning Walk" presents the Naipaulian dilemma of the 'idea' of the homeland as opposed to its reality and the process of rejection and acceptance:

Barbaric city sick with slums
Its hawkers, beggar iron lunged
And child like masses many tongued
Whose wages are in words and crumbs. (119)

Alone he waited for the sun
And felt his blood a sluggish stream
Why had it given him no light
His native place he could not shun. (119)

Faced with this dilemma, alienated Ezekiel wonders of he is "among the men of straw/ who think they go which way they please" (119). The solution comes in the last stanza with the realization that the past is irretrievable:

His past is like a muddy pool
From which he cannot hope for words
The city wakes, where fame is cheap
And he belongs, an active fool. (120)

The use of the word "active" underlines a conscious effort on the part of the poet in order to belong. All diasporas are characterized by a yearning for the homeland and a long engagement with coming to terms with their irretrievable loss. Ezekiel had gone through all these phases in his attempt to break free from India and go abroad, and later, in his decision to return to India and "belong". This transitory phase is common to the diasporic sensibility and can be observed in great detail in the works of Ezekiel and Naipaul. At the time of the publication of *An Area of Darkness,* Ezekiel was going through the phase of "acceptance" while Naipaul was going through the phase of "rejection".

In *An Area of Darkness*, Naipaul records that "Anger, compassion and contempt were aspects of the same emotion which were without value because they could not endure, and achievement could begin only with acceptance" (88). In "Naipaul's India and Mine", Ezekiel states his belief in the value of acceptance:

> I believe in anger, compassion and contempt, they are not without value. I believe in acceptance that incorporates all three, makes use of them I am incurably critical and sceptical. That is what I am in relation to India also. And to myself I find it does not prevent the growth of love. (88)

Ezekiel concludes his essay by pointing out that alongside all the squalor and poverty there is enough positive movement in modern India:

> There is some endeavour too, in modern India, which need hardly be mentioned as evidence for hope. It is at least as obvious as the poverty and the squalor, physical, social and moral. A book could be written about it which would not have to falsify or exaggerate anything. It might well point the way out of the present Indian confusion. (90)

Twenty-seven years and two books later Naipaul confesses in *India: A Million Mutinies Now*:

> What I hadn't understood in 1962 or had taken too much for granted was the extent to which the country had been remade...restored to itself. (517)
>
> In 27 years I had succeeded in a kind of return journey, shedding my Indian nerves, abolishing the darkness that separated me from my ancestral part. (516)

Naipaul's *India: A Million Mutinies Now* is the book that Ezekiel had intended in his essay—a book that "does not have to falsify or exaggerate" by a writer who is not "uninvolved" with his environment. Thus, Ezekiel's critique of Naipaul should be seen as an engagement with the diasporic sensibility anticipating the Naipaulian shift which was to take place years later and not as a testimonial that certifies that in his defence of India, Ezekiel is as Indian as the rest.

Works Cited

Ezekiel, Nissim. "Naipaul's India and Mine." *New Writing in India*. Ed. Adil Jussawalla. Baltimore: Penguin Books, 1974: 71-90. Print.

———. *Collected Poems 1952-1988*. New Delhi: OUP, 1989. Print.

Gowda, H.H. Anniah. "Naipaul in India." *Literary Half Yearly*, 11.2 (1970): 163-10. Print.

Naipaul, V.S. *An Area of Darkness*. 1964; London: Penguin Books, 1968. Print.

———. *Finding the Centre*. 1984; London: Penguin Books, 1985. Print.

———. *India: A Million Mutinies Now*. 1990; London: Vintage, 1998. Print.

———. *The Enigma of Arrival*. London: Penguin Books, 1987. Print.

Narasimhaiah, C.D. "Somewhere Something has Snapped." *Literary Criterion*, 6.4 (1965): 83-96. Print.

Singh, K. Natwar. "Unhappy Pilgrim." *New York Times Book Review*, 11 July 1965: 35. Print.

15

Contamination Perpetrated by Diaspora

Amod Kumar Rai

Kiran Desai, daughter to the profound woman writer Anita Desai, revitalises with her works a literary tradition which has long been buried somewhere. The tradition was shaped and developed much by her own mother who at times was very much close to the coveted award of booker but unfortunately never picked it up for her countrymen. Kiran Desai, however, was born to make history and she did it by grabbing the award in a very young age and became the youngest woman writer ever to win the prestigious Man Booker Prize for Fiction. Kiran Desai first came to literary attention when Salman Rushdie mentioned her in his work *Mirrorwork: Fifty Years of Indian Writing* in 1998. Her first work *Hullabaloo in the Guava Orchard* nabbed people's attention and the second work made her a celebrity all around the world. *The Inheritance of Loss* is set partly in India and partly in the U.S.A. (explores at a deeper level, the consequences of the introduction of a western element into a non-western country, which happened during a British colonial period in India, and is happening again with India's improved relationship with America from the last decade of the 20th century. The book unfolds a story of migration and lives being made over. In page after page, one finds the stories of Indian village life and of her people's attempts to grapple with modernity side by side with the stories of Illegal immigrants in a modern-center of globalized politics and economy like New York. But Kiran Desai's India is largely an imagined country as she had left her homeland as a school girl in her early teens. She chose to write about the 1980s because that was the India that was most familiar to her, the place where she had lived until she was fourteen. But she was aware of the fact that the country she knew has changed so much so that she finds herself at a disadvantage and feels that the subject really belongs to Indian writers living in India.

In her novel Indian people are afflicted by incurable poverty and privation. Their minds are filled with anguish and anger that result from non-fulfillment of their basic needs and that lead them to resort to terrorist violence. On the other hand, there are people who wish to leave the country because of poverty, mal-development and lack of opportunities. But many of them find it difficult to be happy and successful in the West. Biju, the cook's son, is a representative of these Indians who live miserably both at home and abroad and whom happiness eludes forever. To people like Biju, India is a backward, an underdeveloped and uncivilized place where to live happily is difficult. Like other diasporic writers, Kiran Desai too goes in bringing down this ugly face of the country as it entertains the Western readers more than the Indians.

Kiran Desai, the winner of the prestigious Man Booker Prize, 2006, for her second novel. *The Inheritance of Loss* (2006) explores colonial neurosis, multiculturalism, modernity, immigrants' bitter experiences, insurgency and the game of possession, gender-bias, racial discrimination, changing human relations, impact of globalization, Puran-type delineation of the North-East of India, postcolonial chaos and despair, ethno-racial and historical relationships between people from different cultures and backgrounds. Love, longing and losses are dexterously handled in a humane manner articulating diasporic experiences of the novelist who is an Indian citizen but a permanent resident of America. Kiran Desai is deeply interested in India—the India of 1980s—honestly represents the mixed image of India. The present paper endeavors to bring forth the various aspects of India and its people. Desai observes everything through the "lens of being Indian", without that perspective, she acknowledged, "she can't write" (wiki/kirandesai). During

Jaipur Literature Festival, in an interview she expressed her pleasant experience: "It's best time to be an Indian writer.... I do know that present day India isn't really my subject" (*The Times of India*, Jan. 22, 2007). It was only when she began to writing about the immigrant experience in New York that she realized she would have to return to India. But she finds India has changed, it belongs to the Indian author living in India. The subjects belong to them. She goes back to India of the 1980s. It is this feeling of being caught between two continents that infuses the novel. "At times it appears to rejoice in the intermingling of cultures; at others it seems to inspire a wistful melancholy. But, re-discovering her Indian-ness was vital to her, she tells Laura Barton" (*Guardian*, Thursday, October 12, 2006). Consequently, she makes the novel an Indian treating subjects concerning Indian life in India as well as in abroad. She superbly elaborates all these in highly experimented English, i.e. uses Indian slangs, dialectic words, abuses of various regions, vulgar and obscene expressions, colloquial vocabulary—introduce an element of naturalism; highly congenial to image and sensibility of India.

Politically, India was hit by insurgency. It imposed a big threat to law and order. Entire novel is set in the backdrop of insurgency rising in the North-East, i.e. GNLF movement which disrupted the normal life, tourism, business and peace. Out of fifty-three chapters of the novel more than eighteen chapters are exclusively devoted to describe insurgency to highlight the dismal picture of the region. Poverty, unemployment, socio-economic backwardness, xenophobia, discriminatory policies and the government's apathy to seek remedies are deeply rooted in the separatist movements rampant in the whole country. No part is spared; it's alarming and anticipates disastrous consequences: "Separatist movement here, separatist movement there, terrorists, guerillas, insurgents, rebels, agitators, instigators, and all they learn from one another, of course—the Neps have been encouraged by the Sikhs and their Khalistan, by ULFA, NEFA, PLA; Jharkhand, Bodoland, Gorkhaland; Tripura, Mizoram, Manipur, Kashmir, Punjab, Assam..." (128-29). The close nexus among these makes the political problem more grim and intractable. Desai curtly blames the policy-makers for these violent movements: "This state making, the biggest mistake that fool Nehru made. Under his rules any group of idiots can stand up demanding a new state and get it, too...it all started with Sikkim. The Neps played such a dirty trick and began to get grand ideas—now they think can do the same thing again" (128). The genesis of GNLF Movement is narrated by a man clambered up on the bench:

> in 1947, brothers and sisters, the British left granting India her freedom, granting the Muslims Pakistan, granting special provisions for the scheduled castes and tribes—Except us. EXCEPT US, The Nepalis of India. At that time, in April of 1947, the Communist Party of India demanded a Gorkhaland, but the request was ignored...we are laborers on the tea plantations, coolies dragging heavy loads, soldiers. And are we allowed to become doctors and government workers, owners of tea plantations? No! We are kept at the level of servants. (158)

"Gorkhaland for Gorkhas" (7) is the motto of the movement; the activists work on universal guerilla fashion. Kukri, sickles, axes, kitchen knaves, spade or any kind of firearm they look for to make the movement more and more violent to force the government to grant statehood. Assam, Nagaland, Mizoram and Punjab were on fire with the assassination of Indira Gandhi; and Sikhs with their kanga, kachha, etc., still wishing "to all a sixth K, Khalistan, their own country in which to live with the other five Ks" (108). Socio-cultural and political identity and quest for autonomy furthers and kindles the fire of agitation. Indian Nepalese are fed up being treated like the minority in a place where they were the majority. "They wanted own country or at least their own state, in which to manage their own affairs" (9). Gyan's involvement in the separatist movement is the reflection of young Indians deep-rooted frustration, for which Gyan even sacrifices the love of Sai. A feeling of "martyrdom crept over him" (175) and he was overwhelmed and swayed by its vortex. Arson, looting, strike, bundh and the violent reactions were the commonplaces of the time. The novel opens and ends with insurgency. In the opening chapter, Jemu's house is besieged and a hunting rifle is plundered; chapter fifty-two ends with Biju robed by Gurkha mercenaries and chased by dogs in the jungle. The partition of India and the emergence of Pakistan is indeed, Desai poignantly reacts: "First heart attack to our country...that has never been healed" (129).

The novel portraits the Indian society as poverty-stricken; moreover illiteracy, unemployment, xenophobia, cultural conflicts, traditional values, customs, practices; and multiplicity of languages, religions, faiths constitute the very structure of the society in which the novelist is deeply interested. Though she draws a dismal picture of the Indian society, she has a humanistic approach—even characters, i.e. Jemu, Sai, Gyan, Biju, Cook, Loha, Noni, Booty, Potty and Bela all are helpless and feel inferior by their subject position—Desai, very candidly and human manner treats them. Poverty is the root cause of GNLF movement and migration. Gyan's involvement in GNLF movement and frustration caused by the extreme polarities he witnesses between the poor and the rich brings drastic changes in his attitude and love. He is upset to undertake long walk in the cold for the small amount of money the judge paid him. It maddened him that: "People lived here (Cho Oyu) in this enormous house and property, taking hot baths, sleeping alone in spacious rooms...cutlets and peas dinner" (162). He is born of poverty. Cook and Biju epitomize the distress of common men. Biju migrates to America because he is badly hit by poverty; he bears every kind of exploitation for the sake of money, cook renders yeoman services to Jemu. On the contrary, Jemu humiliates and kicks the Cook. It pained Sai's heart to see how poverty has worked on Cook: "A poverty-stricken man growing into an ancient at fast-forward.

Compressed childhood, lingering old age.... There was age in his temperament, his kettle, his clothes, his kitchen, his voice, his face, in the undisturbed dirt, the undisturbed settled smell of a lifetime of cooking, smoke, and kerosene" (19). Cook advises Biju: "Just make sure you are saving money" (18) so that they might overcome poverty. Sai's journey from Dehradoon to Darjeeling notices the panorama of village life and India looks as old as ever; realistic description arrests our attention: "Women walked by with firewood on their heads, too poor for blouses under their saris.... It was early in the morning and the railways tracks were lined with rows of bare bottoms... defecating onto the tracks, rinsing their bottoms with water from a can" (30). Chapatis, jalebis, samosa, fish, chips, pakora, tea, chhang, laddoos, chooran, srikhand, fresh milk, etc. figure in regular meals of the society gradually experiencing transition and replacing them with Angrezi Khana. But all over Kalimpong modernity began to fail.

The novel is a brilliant study of Indian culture—the culture in its transitional phase. Changes are brought out by "colonial neurosis," craze for the Western values, manners, language and glamorous lifestyle, impact of modernization, consumerism, globalization and deep-rooted reaction to indigenous values which failed to sustain life. Characters feel inferior, bounded and defeated by their Indian heritage confronted with colonialism; consequently, they develop grotesque complexes which mar their mutuality and reciprocal relationship. Jemu, Lola, Pixie, Noni, Biju, Cook, Sai, Gyan all are generic, reflect the pain of transition. Despite political freedom, cultural slavery is directly manifested through these characters. They are in a "to be or not to be" position; fail to assimilate new culture and give up original culture in totality. There remains identity crisis which most of the Indians face despite postcolonial reactions in which endeavour is to revitalize indigenous culture and its values. Jemu originally belongs to Piphit, goes to Cambridge for higher studies, is selected in I.C.S., becomes a judge. In this entire process of making, he goes on adopting the West as a model of excellence; he sacrifices his native values. He even changes the name of his desi wife Beta to Nimi; condemns her for her socio-cultural practices; whereas Sai, the granddaughter is commended because she is a Westernized-Indian brought up by commended because she is finest example of an Anglophile—"being a foreigner in his own country..." (29). Jemu and Sai are type of "estranged Indian living in India" (210). Gyan also satirizes: "You (Jemu and Sai) are like slaves, that's what you are, running after the West, embarrassing yourself" (163). Biju stands for young crazy men of the Third World who dream a plan to go to for money making unflinchingly, they sacrifice original culture and social conventions. When Biju gets a full timer waiter position in New York, he sends reactions to his father:

> "Uniform and food, and the owner is not from India. He is from America itself" (14). He works for the Americans, the Cook reports the contents of Biju's letter to everyone as a thing of pride and high honour in the society. Gyan is also intimidated by Jemu's affluence, very English accent and superior ways. Lola, Noni, Pixie and Mrs. Sen are also camouflaged by British ways. Lola advises her daughter Pixie to leave India because "India is a sinking ship...the doors won't stay open forever...." (47)

Multiculturalism is another characteristic feature of Indian society. Jemu, Sai, Biju, Cook, Lola, Noni, Booty, Potty, Gyan, Mr. and Mrs. Mistry belong to different cultural backgrounds. Desai herself inherited multiculturalism from her parents and grandparents. Her maternal grandmother was a German; grandfather was a refugee from Bangladesh. Her paternal grandparents came from Gujarat, and her grandfather was educated in England. Although she has not lived in India since she was 14, she returns to the family home in Delhi every year. She maintains convivial attitude to all cultures and mildly exposes the vanity and hypocrisy imbibed in them.

Immigration problem is one of the most striking problems. Most of the Indians and Third World citizens face such problem in Europe and America. Desai herself has spent more than twenty years in America, she still holds on Indian passport, struggling to get American citizenship, increasingly, she too is unsure that she would really want to surrender her citizenship. It was her own experience and intimate talks with immigrants in America she could highlight the problem so emphatically. Biju, Saeed, Harish Harry, Saran, Jeev, Rishi, Asian working in America and Europe exemplify the bitter experiences of the immigrants. Father Booty is another example of illegal immigrant who lives in India for forty-five years, while he has the visa for two weeks only. Later he is forced to leave the country. Biju spends his early days working as waiter in New York soon there was "green card check" (16) on employees. He was relieved by the manager, who advised him: "just disappear quietly..." (16). Saeed applied for the immigration lottery each year, but Indians were not allowed to apply hence Biju continued to dodge authorities, moving from one ill-paid job to another for thirty years. "He is frightened to die illegal in America and never saw their families, not for ten years, twenty, thirty, never again" (99). He is overwhelmed by fugitive role, nostalgic reminiscences and racial discrimination; so he is disillusioned by the West. Immigrants' painful experience is embittered by racial discrimination. Biju, whose hopes are very lofty; feels ecstatic when selected to work in New York; soon he encounters with the working conditions, racial discrimination and immigration laws; he is enlisted as "shadow class" (102). Discovers authentic colonial experience how Third World natives are exploited and humiliated in the West: "They drew the lines at crucial junctures" (23) and "on the top, rich colonial, and down below, poor native; Colombian, Tunisian, Ecuadorian.... Above all, the restaurant was French, but below in the kitchen it was Mexican and Indian" (21). Even the glamorous image of the West changes into hatred: "There was a whole world in the basement kitchens in New York" (22). "...the habit of hate had accompanied Biju, and he found that he possessed an awe of White people, who arguably had done India great harm" (77). Jemu also experiences racial discrimination against Indians while he was studying in England and thereafter too. Gyan and GNLF activists find Delhi has adopted discriminatory policies against Gorkhaland.

Nature and landscape description occupies large canvas of the novel; though it extends from Manhattan to Himalayas, it is central to Piphit, Kalimpong, Cho Oyu, and Darjeeling. Topography, scenic beauty, variety of vegetation, changing colours of the sky, patches of clouds, rain, mist, mountain tops, Teesta river, thick forests, cluster of houses, vapour, ice, zig-zag roads and seasonal changes, etc. define nature in the novel. It is sensuous beauty which delights the novelist very much, simultaneously, it is contrasted with rising insurgency and it's violent outbreak disrupting normal life. Her treatment of nature is highly poetic and Wordsworthian finding deeper import in it. The novel opens with nature description: All day, the colours had been those of dusk, mist moving like a water creature across the great flanks of mountains possessed of ocean shadows and depths. Briefly visible above the vapor, "Kanchenjunga was a plume of snow blown high by the storms at its summit" (1). Desai's observation is very keen, acute and specific; even the different parts of a tree embody sensuous beauty as well as represent the psychic conditions of the inhabitants: "Kanchenjunga glowed macabre, trees stretched away on either side, trunks pale, leaves black, and beyond, between the pillars of the trees, a path led to the house" (19). Sometimes, she juxtaposes and blends together various objects and presents an elaborate portrayal, free from "pathetic fallacy" (phrase coined by John Ruskin to signify fidelity between object and its delineation). The vicinity of Cho Oyu is marked by it:

> ...a water climate, a rusty green landscape, creaking and bobbing in the wind. They drove past teas stalls on stilts, chicken being sold in round cane baskets, and Durga Puja goddesses being constructed in shacks...paddy fields and warehouses...to the right, the Teesta river came leaping at them between white banks of sand. Space and sun crashed through the window.... By the riverbank, wild water racing by, the late evening sin in polka dots through the trees, they parted company. To the east was Kalimpong barely managing to stay on the saddle between the Deolo and the Ringkingpong hills. To the west was Darjeeling, skidding down the Singalila mountains...not a street light anywhere in Kalimpong, and the lamps in the houses were so dim you saw them only as you passed, forest making sss tseu tsts seuuu sounds. (30-31)

Her involvement in nature and landscapes of India confirms her unending interest and diasporic articulation. Unlike Wordsworth, Desai hardly tries to divinize nature or feels the presence of God anywhere. She investigates parallel development in changing seasons and incidents of violence: "The incidents of borrow grew, through the changing of the seasons, through winter and a flowery spring, summer, then rain and winter again. Roads were closed, there was curfew every night, and Kalimpong was trapped in its own madness. You couldn't leave the hillsides; nobody even left their houses if they could help it but stayed locked in and barricated" (279). Nature is, here, subservient to human emotions and actions, i.e., force and meaning and aesthetic beauty as well. *The Sunday Express* has eulogized Desai's portrayal of nature and landscapes and masterly use of language: "Descriptions of the mountains and the people of Kalimpong, the changing seasons and the inner mindscapes of her characters are mesmerizing; her use of language is virtuoso, and her ideas sparkle" (Courtesy: Internet).

The novel is essentially a study of losses—loss of culture, loss of identity, loss of human relations, loss of emotional binding, loss of human values, loss of rationality, loss of peace and harmony, loss of human beings' faith in each other, etc. Sense of loss is an integral part of every character's life; they are insecure, and unmoored, struggling to survive in the modern world, unsure of whether they will ever see the benefits of globalization; characters unnecessarily feel inferior due to their Indian heritage. Historical events have deep personal import that last people's lifetime and even beyond. Jemu who originally hails from Piphit; goes to Cambridge for higher studies, selected in I.C.S. and becomes a judge. He is so much impressed and immersed in Western values, he loses his original Indian identity and feels like a "foreigner in his own country" (29). He is one of those ridiculous Indians who can't rid themselves of what they had broken their souls to learn and whose Anglophilia can only turn into self-hared. These Indians are also unwanted anachronism in postcolonial India, where long-suppressed peoples have begun to awaken to their dereliction to express their anger and despair; GNLF movement is an outburst of that reaction and Gyan's xenophobia is rooted in it. Jemu can't free himself from "colonial neurosis" (46). He envied the English. He loathed Indians. He worked at being English with the passion of hatred and for what he would become, he would be despised by absolutely everyone, English and Indians both (119). Jemu loses peace by the arrival of Sai and Biju and GNLF activities; strongly misses the glorious past and Mutt for whom he laments loudly. Due to insurgency North-East loses indigenous cultural values. In the process of academic learning in a convent school Western Christian values enter into her blood. Though she remains full of contradictions (30) she also suffers from identity crisis. The biggest loss she feels profoundly is the love of Gyan. Biju who goes to New York with bright hopes, soon discovers authentic colonial experience how the Third World poor natives are exploited and humiliated in the West: They drew the lines at crucial junctures (23) and on the top, rich colonial, and down below, poor native; Columbian, Tunisian, Ecuadorian.... Above all, the restaurant was French, but below in the kitchen it was Mexican and Indian (21). White men also shout: Uloo ka Pattha son of an owl, lay down son-of-a-bitch Indian (23). Even the glamorous picture of the West changes into hatred: There was a whole world in the basement kitchens of New York (22). He also faces tough and discriminatory immigration laws in America, fails to procure green card; listed shadow class (102) of illegal immigrants in New York and spends thirty years time dodging the authorities, moving from one ill-paid job to another. His bitter experience in America and home sickness compels him for homecoming. Even in his own country he finds total loss of peace, law and order. He is robbed by GNLF activists and chased by dogs. Biju emerges as a generic figure, represents young crazy men of the Third World who dream a plan to go to the West and face tough ordeals there. Lola, Noni, Pixie and Mrs. Sen are also trapped by British ways. Lola advises her daughter Pixie, a BBC reporter: "Better leave (India) sooner than later.... India is a sinking ship. Don't want to be pusy, darling, sweetie, thinking of your happiness only, but the doors won't stay open for ever" (47). Lola and Noni are publicly humiliated by Pradhan of GNLF, violate the dignity of genteel women while both the sisters go to complain against encroachment in Mon Ami. Loss of dignity and dreamland (Mon Ami) make them helpless. Father Booty, who runs a dairy in Kalimpong, spends forty-five years as an illegal immigrant, while he has the visa for two weeks only. Later he is forced to leave the country. Consequently, he lost everything but his memories (257). Gyan sacrifices the love of Sai for his Gorkhaland. Cook loses his honour when he is cruelly beaten by Jemu on the missing of Mutt. Almost all of Desai's characters have been stunted by their encounters with the West.

Kiran Desai makes the novel Indian—both by contents and form. Whether its topography, idyllic beauty or the elaborate description of insurgency, description of mountains, mist, changing seasons, Kalimpong, Cho Oyu, Darjeeling, Piphit, immigration problem, culture conflicts, the inhabitants or the inner mindscapes of characters, Desai frees herself from the stereotyped Euro-centric models and honestly and powerful technique to create the manifest sense of Indian-ness. She prefers American English and tries to make it Indianized. She has encountered with American and British writers of English and studied creative writing at Columbia University. Subsequently, she has experimented a lot with the language. Use of popular slangs, dialectic words, abuses of various regions, vulgar and obscene expressions introduce an element of naturalism; Indian vocabulary, Indian metaphors and imagery, etc. are highly supportive to fill up the portrayal of picture and sensibility of India. Indian vocabulary creates a congenial atmosphere to transport the reader into that realm where India resides.

Every chapter in the novel begins with topical line, italicized; thereafter, the novelist elaborates and illustrates the topic. Chapter one "All Day" introduces major characters, secluded life in Kalimpong, Kanchenjunga, Judge, Sai, Gyan, Biju Cook, Mutt, insurgency in North-East and romance of Gyan and Sai. Chapter three "All the Way in America" elaborates immigrants bitter experiences, disillusionment and racial discrimination. Chapter seven "Oh, Grandfather more Lizard than Human" focuses on Jemu's character—dehumanized and Anglophile. Chapter nine "Oh my God" introduces Lola, Noni and their craze for the West and changing identity. Chapter fifteen "In Kalimpong" topography and scenic beauty of the region is highlighted. Chapter twenty "Gyan and Sai" deals with love and insurgency. Chapter twenty-seven "Moody and Restless" expresses the unrest of Gyan. Chapter forty "The Incidents of Horror Grew" portraits the increasing insugency in Kalimpong.

Use of popular slangs, dialectic words, abuses of various regions, vulgar and obscene expressions are frequently used: nakhara, pakora, buzoor, chhang, mia-bibi, mithai, pitaji, Angrezi Khana, salwars, kamaal hai, Baap rei, laddoos, dhotis, jhora, pallu, Budhoo, choksee, Neps, Namaste, aiyiye, baethiye, khaiye, dhanayawad, shukuria, chapattis, jalebi, haveli, tika, chokra, murga-murgi, bania, dhobi, hubshi, haat, atta, srikhand, kundan, peepal, choolah, rasta roko, phata phat, Bilkul Bekar, Jai Gorkha, Saag, bhai, Goras, ghas phoos, goondas, sukhtara, susu fucking oil, ber, chooran, jamun, tatti, roti-namak, gadhas, murdabad, paranthas, tamasha, chappals, desi, etc.

Even full length expression figure significantly: "Humara kya hoga, hai hai, humara kya hoga" (8), "Bar bar karta rahata hai" (11), "O! Yeh ladki zara si deewani lagti hai..." (51), "Angrez ki tarah, Angrez jaise," (105), "Rasta roko" (107), "Gas maar rah hai"(217), "Jai Gorkha" (7), etc.

Abuses and vulgar expressions: "Sooar ka bachha," "uloo ka pattha" (23), "sala" (148), "bephkuph" (182), "bhenchoot" (287), "sala manhoos" (289), and "gadhas" (297), etc. Indian imagery and metaphors are also used: "cheeks like two Simla apples" (262); the technical terms also get place, i.e. "224k" (45). Obscene descriptions read like a blue film; for Desai they are not obscene or pornographic. She narrates them very candidly. Jemu's sex with his wife Bela reads like this: "...he clamped down on her, tussled her to the floor, and as more of that perfect rose complexion, blasted into million mates, came filtering down, in a dense frustration of lust and fury-penis uncoiling, mottled purple-black as if with rage, blundering, uncovering the chute he had heard rumour of—he stuffed his way ungracefully into her" (169).

The author's chef d'euvre, *The Inheritance of Loss,* however, is a work far more plausible than her maiden venture and analyzes confidently with equal ease the lacerating immigrant experience of the non-Nepalese in Darjeeling, Kalimpong and other neighbouring hilly areas holding forth with fortitude and resilience against the Gorkha National Liberation Front's demand for Gorkhaland and the ordeals faced by the Indians and nationals of other Third World countries in the capacity of expatriates making a sincere bid at self-actualization and assimilation in the country of adoption.

Robin Cohen in *Global Diasporas* defines diaspora as a community of people who have settled outside their natal country but acknowledge their loyalties towards and ties with the country of their origin by voicing or implying a sense of co-ethnicity with the people of their country back home as fellow members of their diaspora. Victor Ramraj in his essay Diasporas and Multiculturalism discriminates between immigrant/exile and expatriate writing and diasporic writing by asserting that immigrant writing would be more inclined towards the contemporary experience in the host society whereas diasporic works are likely to more preoccupied with the idea of the deserted or imagined homeland. Kiran Desai has adeptly blended in her later novel immigrant and diasporic writing for on the one hand she depicts the problems confronted by immigrants like Biju in the United States and on the other, she delineates the heart-rending pangs of remaining away from one's homeland and being discriminated against for having permanently settled in a geographical area one does not belong to. Alienation and estrangement are inherent aspects of the migrant situation in which the individual's identity is torn between the old and new worlds of experience. Immigration itself being a facet of post-colonialism, relevant here is the statement drawn from *The Empire Writes Back*: "a major feature of postcolonial literature is the concern with placement and displacement". The ramifications of these two terms, "placement" and "displacement" are multiple and the psychocultural issues involved are many.

Today, American writing in English including the works of the Indian diaspora has evolved into an amazingly diverse canvas catering to the experiences of people from different ethnic, racial and immigrant groups that are today incorporated into the social edifice of the United States of America. Kiran Desai, an established member of the Indian diaspora in the United States, makes the best of this prevalent Inheritance of Loss a significant chunk of the history of India when inordinate insurgency born of the Nepalese Movement during the 1980s perpetrated heinous crimes on the pretext that the community was being persecuted and tormented in Bengal. They were not prepared to settle for anything less than statehood, a homeland in and around Darjeeling and Kalimpong. The GNLF men assaulted affluent Bengalis and people from other states who they believed had encroached upon their land. One such target was Jemubhai Patel, the Gujarati judge who had chosen to settle in Kalimpong after his retirement. Born in pre-independence colonial India, Jemubhai had gone to England for advanced studies and had come back to India to serve under the British Government. He was totally detached from his family and there was no emotional bond that drew him to his wife and his only daughter. He lived alone in his old bungalow, Cho Oyu, which he had acquired in Kalimpong. His only companion here was his cook, who still, like his master, laboured largely under the influence of colonialism, and who, after having lost five mango trees to his brother in a court case, had left his village in Uttar Pradesh to work for the judge with whom he still remained. The only person who joined Jemubhai later in Cho Oyu was his granddaughter, Sai, who arrived in Kalimpong after the unfortunate demise of her parents.

Another aspect of the immigrant experience is that of Biju, the only son of the cook who had migrated to the United States in the hope of a "better life". The cook had been lured by the prospect of a "legal employment in the U.S.A." and had manipulated some counterfeit recommendations for his son, which had finally helped Biju in being selected at the interview. At this achievement the cook was elated and started comparing himself with Mrs Sen whose daughter was also in America. To everyone he met he proudly announced:

> My son works in New York. He is the manager of a restaurant business...New York. Very big city. The cars and buildings are nothing like here, in that country there is enough food for everybody. One day soon, my son will take me.

The cook, however, was not aware of the exact nature of Biju's work in America. Being ignorant of his son's travails and anxieties abroad, he generously recommended to him the names of some of the local boys aspiring to go to America and asked the former to help them in getting jobs. Ironically, he was blissfully oblivious of the dire circumstances under which his own son worked to keep body and soul together.

Mrs Sen thought herself privileged in having a daughter who worked in America and did not forget to take a dig at her neighbour, Lola, whose daughter worked in England in the capacity of a BBC newsreader: "All these people who went to England are now feeling sorry." For the cook, however, the difference between America and England remained vague. He was contented with whatever his son and many others like him had acquired a tourist visa to go to America they were treated as illegal migrants after the expiry of the visa and were under stress from all sides. They could neither live honorably as immigrants nor relinquish their aspirations and come back to their native country. Biju too, embroiled in this typical predicament had no standing and identity of his own. Like a fugitive on the run he had to switch from one job to another lest he be discovered and penalized as an illegal immigrant who had stayed on longer than permitted by law. Subjected to trenchant remarks that pierced his heart Biju had to labour under indignities that reminder him of the plight of the colonized way back in the past. He worked in numerous hotels and restaurants—French, Mexican, Italian, Indian—and invariably had to share a room downstairs with the other workers, some of whom, especially a Pakistani, he never got along with:

> The sound of their fight had traveled up the flight of steps and struck a chunky note, and they might upset the balance, perfectly first world on top, perfectly third world twenty-two steps below.

The contempt for the inhabitants of the Third World countries is clearly evident. To all to the humiliation the wife if the proprietor of the Italian restaurant, Pinocchio, disdainfully observed that Biju "smelled" and the latter had finally to search for a new for the lady was unappeasable:

> She had hoped for poorer parts of Europe-Bulgarians perhaps, or Czechoslovakians. At least they might have something in common with them like religion or skin colour, grandfathers who ate cured sausages and looked like them.

Biju very soon realized that people from the Third World countries were engaged in a losing battle for existence. Braving the severe cold in America was another front for which Biju had to brace himself:

> Biju smelled the first of the snow and found that it had the same procking, difficult smell that existed inside the freezer; he felt the Thermocol scrunch of it underfoot. On the Hudson, the ice cracked lay into pieces, and within the contours of this gray, broken river it seemed as if city's inhabitants were being provided with a glimpse of something far and forlorn that they might use to consider their own loneliness.

Alienation, estrangement, humiliation and bone-chilling frost, all contributed to the sense of utter loneliness experienced by Biju in America. His father's friend, Nandu, whom he had been banking upon for all kinds of help, callously gave him the cold shoulder and dismissed him with the advice that he should go back to India. Biju soon realized the prevalence of a deep divide between the legal and the illegal immigrants and knew that unless and until his immigration was formalized and given a legal sanction, he would not even be able to go back to his native land and would continue being exploited by some restaurant owners like Harish-Harry, who were busy making money at the cost of poor Indians and nationals of other Third World countries who did not have the authorized stamp on their papers. All his dreams melted away in the light of this realization of utter helplessness:

> The green card the green card. Without it may be could not leave. To leave he wanted a green card. This was the absurdity. How he desired the triumphant. After the Green Card Return Home, thirsted for it....

However, as we are made conscious of other characters in the novel, we see that Biju was not alone in his misery:

> ...it WAS so hard and YET there were so many here. It was terribly, terribly hard. Millions risked death, were humiliated hated, lost their families—YET there were so many here.

The novel thus underlines the collapse of the 'American dream' of the poor of the Third World countries like India. These underprivileged people are lured by the hope of better prospects abroad but the 'exile' that they inflict upon themselves to live better, ironically compels them to live in disgrace and wretchedness. The following statement of Santana Haldar corroborates this view,

> Kiran Desai highlights that the process of globalization has its loopholes that the cartographical binaries have collapsed only for a blessed few. The poor people of the third world countries who dream of a better future and are lured by the affluence of the American society have no place in the world of their dream. They are compelled to suffer in their homeland and the exile they opt for only increases their suffering.

The present study focuses on the mode in which Desai shows how the immigrants of the Third World countries are maltreated and an unnerving consciousness of being rootless. The fact that the cook's son, Biju, and all other illegal immigrants quarters of a building, "at the bottom of Harlem" is indicative of the subservient, menial status assigned to them. Like a spurned, rebuffed, jettisoned derelict, Biju makes his way to the Queen of Tarts bakery in the wee hours of the morning,

> watching for the cops who sometimes came leaping out: where are you going and what are you doing with whom at what time and why?

But immigration operated independently of Police, the better, perhaps, to bake the morning bread, and Biju fell, again and again, through the crackers in the system. The indignities suffered by Biju in the United States belied his father's hopes of experiencing a sense of pride and achievement on the former's return home.

In the *Inheritance of Loss*, Kiran Desai perceptively depicts the lives of the gamut of Indian immigrants in the U.S.A.—the affluent and the successful as well as the poor and the hunted—and has tried to bring alive the drama of the erosion of identity in the case of those who have no claims over being minions of Lady Luck. The tension that prevails in the sensitive mind of an immigrant between the two socio-cultural environments and between the feelings of *rootlessness* and nostalgia and the desire to assimilate the new way of life leaves him with a lacerated self trying to piece itself together. Bharati Mukherjee in *Wife* and Anita Desai in *Cry, The Peacock,* both explore the inner space of near-neurotic immigrants abroad but Kiran Desai in the novel understudy is different in that her purpose is to expose the inhuman and discriminatory attitude of the American towards the poorer section of immigrants. Generally however, all immigrants to Western countries, be it Canada, U.S.A. or England to quote Bharati Mukherjee, are "lost souls, put upon and pathetic" and they can be seen...surrendering little bits of self every year, clutching the souvenirs of an ever-retreating past you'll never belong, anywhere.

Whether cultures are inherited or consciously adopted as in the case of the migrant status, basic problems of the definition of identity are inescapable. As Paula M.L. Moya puts it in the introduction to the work, *Reclaiming Identity*:

> .... The significance of identity depends partly on the fact that goods and resources are still distributed according to identity categories. Who we are—that is, who we perceive ourselves or are perceived by others to be—will significantly affect our life chances: where we can live, whom we will marry (or whether we can marry) and what kinds of educational and employment opportunities will be available to us.

This is very true in the light of the identity crisis faced by the underprivileged section of the immigrations in America that Kiran Desai portrays in *The Inheritance of Loss.*

Another aspect of Kiran Desai's novel, *The Inheritance of Loss,* is her pre-occupation with Indian history, like Rushdie's in his fiction. The strains of complexity in her treatment of history are evident from the fact that the human drama in the novel is played out against the backdrop of the insurgency born of the rise of the Nepalese Movement during the 1980s, a chunk of India's recent past. The theme of immigration pertaining to Saeed—Saeed's and Biju's visit to the U.S.A. is equally relevant to the migrant situation that prevails in Kalimpong and Darjeeling with regards to Jemubhai Patel, Sai, the cook, Noni and Lola.

Gyan, the young Nepalese Mathematics tutor, however, finds himself in a dilemma when he has to choose between his beloved, Sai, and his native place, Kalimpong. He is "...caught between two worlds: one promising him Sai and adolescent love 'Free' from history. Free from family demands and the built up debt of centuries" and the other, making him learn through a sense of virility and belonging, "as everyone does in this country, at one time or another, that old *hatreds* are endlessly retrievable".

The ironical tale of a young nation turning against its own people rather than rejoicing at the termination of the colonial rule is deplorable. Unfortunately, despite widespread talk of globalization, to adapt the lines referring to Bapsi Sidhwa's *The Pakistani Bride*, "the differences between the cultural mores of the plains as opposed to those of the peoples who live in the mountains" have re-emerged to draw accentuated borderlines between one region and another and for this, the natives and the immigrants are both responsible for neither group tries to accommodate to the other. The native Nepalese of the Kalimpong and Darjeeling region from the very beginning believed that they had been given a raw deal and justice had not been meted out to them. The immigrants from West Bengal who had settled there were equally unhappy with the conditions that had come to prevail and were now very suspicious of the local Nepalese residents. Lola (Lalita) for instance, voices her suspicion when she exclaims, "I tell you, these Neps cant be trusted. And they don't just rob. They think absolutely nothing of murdering, as well." Robe Pope's words in this context are very illuminating.

> In every domain of language, literature and culture there is an acute tension and sometimes a flat contradiction between globalizing process of standardization and localizing process of differentiation.

Kiran Desai with her priorities rooted firmly in Indian ethics would like to wish away such animosity between any two communities of men and would have peace and amity prevail. For a close realization of this blissful state the following clues to a future standpoint given by Sanjay Solanki in his essay, "Past, Present and the Future in *The Inheritance of Loss*," may help:

> The postcolonial and multicultural perspectives entail a subtle reconfiguring of attitudes: no extreme and facile stance can overnight purge us of our colonial hangover and undo the material intellectual and cultural destruction that came in its wake. Nor formulaic posturing—like Jemu's masochistic Anglophilism or Biju's Anglophobia—can do in a world changing fast. Nor does the situation offer a luxury of glib solutions like the ones Lola, Noni and Mrs. Sen would seem to approve of. To be well placed in this feverish pace of the globalized world, what is required is not the poise, seclusion, nor Macdonaldization of society is the answer, especially for the Asian countries in which poverty is much more concentrated than in the European countries.

Kiran Desai in her novel, *The Inheritance of Loss* (2006) attempts to locate the blurring lines of the history of Indian mental architecture from the colonial rule to the contemporary time. Desai skillfully demonstrates this through the convergence of the tormented past and an indeterminately positioned multicultural/multiethnic present. All through the narrative woven with assorted and generically complex composition, Desai offers a panoramic representation of a constructed reality where individuals are engaged in an incessant search for personal identity. Macrocosm and microcosm in the narrative coalesce to interweave each small event into the plot in terms of construction of an image of the "self" and the "other" that is essentially partial. Through a partial and mimic representation (Bhabha 1994) of the individual Desai's narrative effectively confronts and challenges the murkiness of the individual identity constructed by the colonial discourse *vis-à-vis* agency to induce separation among and to exercise control over members of a culture well-known for peaceful coexistence for centuries in spite of differences. Her subtle examination of boundaries concurs with a concern for hybridist, the issue of individual space, the lineage of colonial past and postcolonial present.

As pointed out by Ashcroft (2005) "the mimicry of the post-colonial subject" can effectively destabilize or subvert the colonial discourse by establishing "an area of considerable political and cultural uncertainty in the structure of imperial dominance" (142). A complete policy of normalization regulates the native population to subliminally construct their own identities as colonial subjects realizing the agenda of the hegemonic power (Foucault 1991; Ashcroft 2005). What emerges in the process is the colonial stereotype instead of autonomous individuals governed by principles of an asymmetrical power relationship. Bhabha's (1994) inveterate argument demonstrates that a refractive encounter between the civilizing agenda and the post-colonial materiality enables subversive and emerging forms of resistance tend to be rectified via the very tools for repression as well as manipulation employed by the colonial discourse. A reverse process is initiated by this, challenging the colonial agenda of creating a stereotype. He points out that the very mechanism that endorses the control and supremacy of the colonial discourse, the fact exposes its inherent vulnerability leading to its ultimate peaceful demise from within. An illustration of colonial imitation exemplifies the destabilization of the restructuring and civilizing mission by the shifting gaze of its punitive double in the gray area between "mimicry" and "mockery" (Bhabha 1994).

Though the process is inverted by means of the reversal of gaze by its "disciplinary double" the mechanism relegates the individual into a constructed subject position that remains the same. By sharing the discursive practice the subversive and emerging position through "the excess or slippage produced by the ambivalence of mimicry" not only ventures forth to discontinue the discourse, but also inculcates in the colonial subject an indeterminacy leading to an "incomplete", "partial" and "virtual" presence (Bhabha 1994). Mimicry becomes both "resemblance and menace" in that the "proliferation of inappropriate objects" ascertaining the strategic failure results in success of the colonial appropriation.

An inescapable sense of inferiority is inculcated in the colonial subject by prolonged subjugation under colonial rule due to uncertain space(s) of individual in the cultural regime. This subsequently shapes and influences the architecture of the mind of several characters in the novel both as postcolonial subjects and the "disciplinary double". The very first chapter of the novel introduces the reader to five important characters in the novel. Whereas Sai, Gyan and Mutt, the dog, are introduced by their names; the judge and the cook are introduced by their respective designations. The judge's claustrophobic preoccupation with his own self is aptly but ironically portrayed by an image of an individual with a chessboard "playing against himself" (1). The anonymous representation of the judge, a major character in the novel who is obsessively preoccupied with his own exiled world, immediately invokes into one's mind the image of the Boss created by Katherine Mansfield in *The Fly*, Sai, throughout the text, exposes a dynamicity of character though her grandfather's stagnant character is projected is the primary token, Gyan, a representative of the insurgent group that invades the household of the judge can be seen as the "disciplinary double" in the narrative that tends to destabilize the discursive practice of the colonial cultural regime.

The leading question in the very beginning of the novel—"(c)ould fulfillment ever be felt as deeply as loss" (2)—sets the introspective and somber tone of the novel. The feeling of inferiority, indeterminacy and uncertainty leads individuals to a quest of identity through participants in the colonial administration or the insurgent movement. The legacy that begins in this narrative with Jemubhai Patel appears to be inherited by members of later generations.

Jemubhai begins his quest for identity from a position of the "other" to become a member of the mainstream by way of putting on a person with an Endeavour to mark the "sameness" with the powerful in him. His futile efforts isolate him from the group he originally belongs to without granting him the much desired membership of the "desired" "civilized" class of the British in India. While Jemubhai's quest for identity is negotiated through adoption of normative parameters of the class of the powerful, Gyan's is negotiated through an apparent (though tentative) expression of resistance and directionless vengeance; while Biju takes resort to subjugation, and his father seeks it in an imagined socio-economic space achieved through father his son's economic prosperity in a country much beyond his own reach. Whereas participation in colonial administration is viewed as a tool of empowerment is seen as empowering for people that Gyan represents. In fact, incidents in Jemubhai's universe are re-enacted in lives of almost all major character in the novel. On several occasions and instincts Gyan is represented as a dichotomy of Jemubhai. Instinctive responses such as misogyny, violence against their respective female counterparts, and identity crisis bind these two characters very closely. The narrative becomes a site for contest of identity issues mediated by individual perceptions of personal identity as well as the identity of the group. Whereas Jemubhai's search for identity creates a prototype subsequently to be represented in Biju's metaphorical as well as physical journey, which is partially Lazarian, Gyan's journey to seek his identity provides the antithesis, i.e. he undertakes the venture not through submission and subjugation but violent resistance through insurgency, a revisited form of subjugation to a new order by inversion of gaze.

Finally Jemubhai's relation and treatment to his wife appears to be a combination of both class and gender issue. Jemubhai looks down upon his wife only because she is a woman and therefore is a subject to subjugation, but also because she represents the non-transformed Indian self—Jemubhai himself is and which he despises so much. Her nonconformist defying presence in his household with her silent resistance to Jemubhai's oppressive behaviour appears as a constant reminder of Jemubhai's powerlessness/impotency, conformity and subjugation that he makes himself subject to for inclusion in the mainstream. Jemubhai's inherent vulnerability is exposed through his act of violence as a result of his inability to face the truth about his own callous submission to the system geared by her comment—"you are the one who is stupid" (304). His violence to his wife exemplifies what Bhabha (1994) identifies as "the narcissistic demand of colonial authority". His wife's comment about his own "stupidity" immediately presents to him "a gaze of otherness" exposing the discernment of "the genealogical gaze" (Bhabha, 1994) shattering the unity of his constructed existence through which he upholds his "sovereignty" (Foucault 1991).

Isolation is a prevalent motif throughout the narrative. In spite of desperate attempts conjugation of individuals to form a unified collective remains unachieved. By the end of the novel each appears to lose something valuable in their own personal lives. Jemubhai loses his dog, the only object of his attachment to this material world; Sai loses her love and probably an unperturbed trust in life; Gyan loses the cause for his resistance; Father Booty loses his long cherished dream and his "home"; the two sisters lose their peaceful musings and leisure; Biju loses all that he saved in his life in "exile" and his father, his imagined space. Though Biju apparently loses all that might have changed his individual identity in the society, the positive note in the novel is maintained through the possibility of redemption of identity marked by Biju's return to his own root without any condition; he represents an individual who exhibits faith in norms of both the external and internal worlds. The journey of each individual in the novel reduplicates Jemubhai's quest the primary concern of which appears to be a search of individual identity as part of the collective. If Jemubhai is the macrocosm in the narrative, each character in the novel plays microcosm to complete a cycle that has been initiated by Jemubhai Popatlal Patel.

This mundane macrocosm in *The Inheritance of Loss* is marked by "partial representation" of individual identity, split personalities, modified motivation, authorized "otherness" personal confusion and indeterminacy devoid of enthusiasm, a sense of individual identity in terms of completeness, security and specified agenda of life, where mockery and mimicry prevails as the order of life and existence (Bhabha 1994). It appears to be the reason why Jemubhai—the representative anglicized Indian bureaucrat—betrays his long cherished 'western', rational and civilized persona (of the authorized other) at the loss of his pedigreed dog Mutt, his only connection to the material world, towards the end of the novel. The unexpected incident of a personal loss compels him to seek refuge in a self-idealized anglicized world in likeness with the colonial system. His characteristic vulnerability as part of his real person is exposed in a circumstance which is sudden, sure and on which, for the second time in his life, he didn't have any control.

The sudden disappearance of Mutt bound Jemubhai, Sai and the cook for their respective 'claustrophobic' sadness due to loss of something valuable in their lives, e.g. Mutt, the only object to attachment to the materialistic world for Jemubhai, an amorous alliance that promised a wide (non-existent) vista to Sai, a certain separation with uncertain fate between the cook and his son, Biju. The joint search party comprised of Jemubhai, Sai and the cook, looking for the dog become a symbolic individual inward quest for each member into their respective personal losses. With full awareness that wistful forgetfulness capacitates one to continue in their routine existence, he succumbs to memory—"One thing Jemubhai learned: a human can be transformed into anything. It was possible to forget and sometimes essential to do so" (308). Jemubhai's delirious rambling, resembling the whine of an insane mind, marks the disintergration of the mimic persona of the "authorised other" and the futility of such an existence. The loss of the dog invokes in his mind his own violent act towards his wife and her subsequent forced acquittal from home as well as his own life. This "fusion of elements" (Eliot 1920) constitutes what Eliot (1920) calls "the substantial unity" of the narrative in the novel—in a miniature and his parts in the reverse.

It is in this gloomy uncertainties of the disintegrating macrocosm of Jemubhai, Biju's arrival in India without any knowledge of the ongoing turmoil in his home reminds one about an individual's return from a space which is cut off from the space she, he belongs to and where such information about the insurgency and consequent changes do not have any information value. His whole existence is alienated from the representational space of the narrative to his lack of knowledge of the state of affairs in the home front, his worldly belongings, even the currency he offers are all very "different" yet his unawareness of it as is Jemubhai. It is because of a lack of awareness of the "different" he appears to be happy after boarding the jeep driven by people who share the same culture and in spite of the "sameness" are going to rob him soon to reduce him to the position of literally an outsider—"he felt so lighthearted to be back, even this journey with these men didn't unsettle him" (311).

In a context devoid of "real" and "complete" identity and individual space, existential insecurity as well as indeterminacy and delusion makes individual to live. This also simultaneously makes the individual (1) seek refuge in denouncement of one's own root and chase impossible as well as distant dreams of an imaged space as in case of Jemubhai and the cook; (2) take resort to violent self-assertion and insurgency as in case of Gyan; (3) uphold silent but strong resistance as in case of Mrs Jemubhai; and (4) discover the futility of vainly ambitious pursuit of a target arbitrarily assigned to an individual externally as in case of Biju. The macrocosm in this novel is a mimic space in which the "self" deprived of autonomy and true representation awaits for a meaningful individual as well as collective identity to make sense of his/her fragmented subjugated self. A strange sense of absurdity characterizes this waiting, symbolizing a barren and callous universe where paranoia prevails without healing and hope. Though individuals appear to be in search of their lost inheritance and identity, they are forbidden by an apprehension about their own constructed self for "...the problems of the road (are) tedious" (315).

The Inheritance of Loss is a narrative of fragmented representative mimic individuals where the issue of identity renders the family as well as individual relationship as a site for contest of assertion of identity and power, thereby ensuring the recognition of partial and mimic representation. So when individuals are confronted with the reality about their being relegated into the domain of helplessness, not only by an external, indifferent and politically motivated system that constructs their identity to exercise control over a group of people stripping in the process of construction of mimic individuals. Consequently, crawling back like parasites, she/he attempts to live afresh, renew life creating for their own self a crippled order, Jemubhai—a stranger to his own people, culture—more distant that anybody else—a non-White carrying out the 'white man's burden' in his own country where he himself is contextualised as a cultural alien—"[h]e had been recruited to bring his countrymen into the modern age, but he could only make it himself by cutting them off entirely, or they would show up reproachful, pointing out to him the lie he had become" (306).

Works Cited

Bhabha, Homi. *The Location of Culture*. London: Routledge, 1994.

Desai, Kiran. *Hullabaloo in Guava Orchard*. London: Faber & Faber, 1998.

———. *The Inheritance of Loss*. New Delhi: Penguin Books India, 2006.

Lakshmi, C.S. *The Face Behind The Mask: Women In Tamil Literature*. New Delhi: Shakti, 1984.

Mishra, Pankaj. NYTimes.com/2006 Book Review.

Naik, M.K. and Shyamala, A. Narayan. *Indian English Literature (1980-2000)*. Delhi: Pencraft International, 2004.

Nimsarakar, P.D. *Kiran Desai: The Novelist*. Creative Writing. New Delhi, 2006.

Nityannandan, Indra. *The Fictional World of Kiran Desai*. Creative Writing, New Delhi, 2007.

http/www.Sawnet.org/books/authors.pp?Desai+Kiran.